Oxford
International
Resources

6

English
Student Book

Emma Danihel

Izabella Hearn

Myra Murby

OXFORD
UNIVERSITY PRESS

OXFORD
UNIVERSITY PRESS

Great Clarendon Street, Oxford, OX2 6DP, United Kingdom

Oxford University Press is a department of the University of Oxford. It furthers the University's objective of excellence in research, scholarship, and education by publishing worldwide. Oxford is a registered trade mark of Oxford University Press in the UK and in certain other countries.

British Library Cataloguing in Publication Data

Data available

ISBN 978-1-38-201989-7

10 9 8 7

Paper used in the production of this book is a natural, recyclable product made from wood grown in sustainable forests. The manufacturing process conforms to the environmental regulations of the country of origin.

Printed in India by Multivista Global Pvt. Ltd

Acknowledgements

The publisher and authors would like to thank the following for permission to use photographs and other copyright material:

Cover: Artwork by Dan Gartman. Photos: **p3(a):** James Devaney/Getty Images; **p3(b):** Smileus/Shutterstock; **p3(c):** Jaroslav Moravcik/Shutterstock; **p8(tl):** Ink Drop/Shutterstock; **p8(tr):** Daniele COSSU/Shutterstock; **p8(b):** Gillmar/Shutterstock; **p9:** Michael Scott/Alamy Stock Photo; **p11:** Suzanne Long/Alamy Stock Photo; **p20:** ImageBROKER/Alamy Stock Photo; **p22:** Stefan Gottermann/Shutterstock; **p23(t):** Edwin Butter/Shutterstock; **p23(m):** Nowaczyk/Shutterstock; **p23(b):** Songquan Deng/Shutterstock; **p24:** Ondrej Prosicky/Shutterstock; **p25:** Yevhenii Chulovskyi/Shutterstock; **p26(tl):** Gurpreet Singh/Hindustan Times/Getty Images; **p26(tr):** AMER HILABI/AFP/Getty Images; **p26(bl):** Harry How/Getty Images; **p26(br):** Hannah Peters/Getty Images; **p27:** Eduard Stelmakh/Shutterstock; **p28:** Berlin-Bild/ullstein bild/Getty Images; **p29:** Bettmann/Getty Images; **p30:** Bettmann/Getty Images; **p31:** Guy Cowdry/Shutterstock; **p32:** Bettmann/Getty Images; **p32:** Compack Background/Shutterstock; **p34:** Ajax News & Feature Service/Alamy Stock Photo; **p35:** matimix/Shutterstock; **p38:** Allen Berezovsky/WireImage/Getty Image; **p40:** James Devaney/Getty Images; **p41:** REUTERS/Alamy Stock Photo; **p42:** Denis Stankovic/Shutterstock; **p44(tl):** Daniel J. Rao/Shutterstock; **p44(tr):** Costazzurra/Shutterstock; **p44(b):** Omer koclar/Shutterstock; **p45(l):** Todd Shoemake/Shutterstock; **p45(r):** idiz/Shutterstock; **p49:** Romolo Tavani/Shutterstock; **p53:** TebNad/Shutterstock; **p54:** Leigh Prather/Shutterstock; **p56(t):** LilKar/Shutterstock; **p56(b):** Radu Razvan/Shutterstock; **p57:** Dougal Waters/DigitalVision/Getty Images; **p62:** Manny DaCunha/Shutterstock; **p66:** Flas100/Shutterstock; **p70:** AF archive/Alamy Stock Photo; **p73:** Flas100/Shutterstock; **p74:** Teo Tarras/Shutterstock; **p75(bkgd):** Morey Milbradt/Alamy Stock Photo; **p74(r):** Claudio Wiens/Alamy Stock Photo; **p74(l):** ROUSSEL BERNARD/Alamy Stock Photo; **p77:** Lanthish Verghese/Shutterstock; **p78:** SpeedKingz/Shutterstock; **p79:** Cherries/Shutterstock; **p81:** canyalcin/Shutterstock; **p83:** Karel Miragaya/123RF; **p85:** Cultura Creative RF/Alamy Stock Photo; **p87:** pio3/Shutterstock; **p88:** Monkey Business Images/Shutterstock; **p90:** Jordon Sharp/Alamy Stock Photo; **p91:** P-fotography/Shutterstock; **p94(bkgd):** Gino Santa Maria/Shutterstock; **p94(tr):** Richard I'Anson/The Image Bank Unreleased/Getty Images; **p94(bl):** Universal Images Group North America LLC/DeAgostini/Alamy Stock Photo; **p94(br):** wavebreakmedia/Shutterstock; **p95:** Simon Kovacic/Shutterstock; **p97:** Windmoon/Shutterstock; **p99:** Anastasia Lembrik/Shutterstock; **p103:** Photographee.eu/Shutterstock; **p104:** Attem/Shutterstock; **p107(t):** Alinute Silzeviciute/Shutterstock; **p107(b):** dezy/Shutterstock; **p108(r):** TCD/Prod.DB/Alamy Stock Photo; **p108(r):** AF archive/Alamy Stock Photo; **p108(bkgd):** Picturebox-uk.com/Alamy Stock Photo; **p109(r):** Everett Collection, Inc./Alamy Stock Photo; **p109(l):** Shutterstock/Maksim Kabakou; **p110:** NagyDodo/Shutterstock; **p113:** eugenegurkov/Shutterstock; **p114(t):** WeAre/Shutterstock; **p118:** Stone36/Shutterstock; **p119:** Nina Firsova/Shutterstock; **p124:** bestfoto77/Shutterstock; **p126(bkgd):** Angela Drury/Corbis; **p126(tl):** Shutterstock; **p126(tr):** Shi Yali/Shutterstock; **p126(bl):** Nature Picture Library/Alamy Stock Photo; **p126(tr):** Bridgeman Images; **p127(l):** Zena Elea/Alamy Stock Photo; **p127(r):** Pool Photo/Alamy Stock Photo; **p128:** Juergen Ritterbach/Photodisc/Getty Images; **p129(t):** KKulikov/Shutterstock; **p129(m):** Roman Spoutil/Shutterstock; **p129(b):** Steve Allen/Shutterstock; **p130:** Jiri Miklo/Shutterstock; **p132, p135(b):** Nature Picture Library/Alamy Stock Photo; **p134:** Wild Shutter/Alamy Stock Photo; **p135(t):** Iakov Filimonov/Shutterstock; **p137:** Layne Kennedy/Corbis Documentary/Getty Images; **p136(bkgd):** Tul R/Shutterstock; **p136:** Compack Background/Shutterstock; **p138:** Robertharding/Alamy Stock Photo; **p139:** Lisa-S/Shutterstock; **p140(t):** bayualam/Shutterstock; **p140(b):** Gts/Shutterstock; **p142:** MIXA Co. Ltd./Getty Images; **p143:** milatas/Shutterstock; **p144(bkgd):** Gumenyuk Dmitriy/Shutterstock; **p144:** Nils Z/Shutterstock; **p145(t):** Anton Starikov/Shutterstock; **p145(br):** Claudio Divizia/Shutterstock; **p145(bl):** Stockbyte/Getty Images; **p147:** Brocreative/Shutterstock; **p148:** Photodisc/Getty Images; **p150:** Flas100/Shutterstock; **p152(bkgd):** Galushko Sergey/Shutterstock; **p152(t):** Michael Ventura/Alamy Stock Photo; **p152(b):** IanDagnall Computing/Alamy Stock Photo; **p153:** Flas100/Shutterstock; **p154(bkgd):** Kaspri/Shutterstock; **p154(b):** Bride Lane Library/Popperfoto/Getty Images; **p157:** Glenn Nagel/Alamy Stock Photo.

Artwork by Dan Gartman, Alfredo Belli, Nina Caniac, Stefan Chabluk, Katriona Chapman, Russ Daff, Jacqui Davis, Dylan Gibson, Alan Marks, Mel Matthews, Gustavo Mazali, Simon Mendes, Dusan Pavlic, Claudia Ranucci, Francesca Resta, Giulia Rivolta, Kimberley Scott, Meilo So, Mike Spoor, Mark Walker, Jan Wijngaard, and Claudia Venturini, Sole Otero, Andy Parker/Oxford University Press, and Q2A Media Services Pvt. Ltd.

Anna Akhmatova: 'Sunbeam' from *The Complete Poems* translated by Judith Hemschemeyer, edited and introduced by Roberta Reeder (Canongate, 1993, 2008). Copyright 1989, 1992, 1997 by Judith Hemschemeyer. Reproduced with permission from Canongate and from Zephyr Press.

Max Fatchen: 'Dragon Dance' from *Let's Celebrate: Festival Poems* compiled by John Foster (Oxford University Press, 1989). Reproduced with permission from Johnson & Alcock for the Estate of M. Fatchen.

David Greygoose: 'It's Only the Storm', first published in *Language in Colour* edited by Moira Andrew (Macmillan Children's Books, 1989). Copyright © David Ward 1989. Reproduced with permission from D. Ward.

John Kitching: 'Historian', first published in Brian Moses (ed): *The Works 2: Poems on Every Subject and For Every Occasion* (Macmillan Children's Books, 2002). Reproduced with permission from T. Dickinson.

Gill Lewis: *White Dolphin* (Oxford University Press, 2010). Reproduced with permission from Oxford University Press.

Alonzo Lopez: 'Celebration' from *Celebration: poems by Alonzo Lopez* (Sundance, 1993). Reproduced with permission from Sundance Newbridge LLC.

Alexander McCall Smith: *Precious and the Monkeys*, published in the USA as *The Great Cake Mystery: Precious Ramotswe's Very First Case: A Number 1 Ladies' Detective Agency Book for Young Readers* (Random House, 2011). Copyright © Alexander McCall Smith 2011, 2012. Reproduced with permission from David Higham Associates for A. McCall Smith.

Spike Milligan: *The 'Veggy' Lion* (Virgin Books, 2006). Reproduced with permission from Spike Milligan Productions Ltd.

Mike Perham: *Sailing the Dream: the Amazing True Story of the School Boy who Sailed Single-handed Around the World* (Bantam, 2010) Copyright © Mike Perham 2010. Reproduced with permission from Andrew Lownie Literary Agency for M. Perham.

Ogden Nash: *Adventures of Isabel* from *Candy is Dandy: The Best of Ogden Nash* (André Deutsch, 1994). Copyright © 1936 by Ogden Nash. Reproduced with permission of Welbeck Publishing Group Ltd and Curtis Brown Ltd for the Estate of Ogden Nash.

Kenn Nesbitt: *My Dad's a Secret Agent* from *The Aliens Have Landed at Our School* (Meadowbrook, 2001). Copyright © 2006. Reprinted by permission of Running Press Kids, an imprint of Hachette Book Group, Inc.

Rainforest Concern: *Conserving Rainforests* adapted from Rainforest Concern website: https://www.rainforestconcern.org/forest-facts/why-are-rainforests-important (Rainforest Concern, 2021). Reproduced with permission from Rainforest Concern.

Any third-party use of this material, outside of this publication, is prohibited. Interested parties should apply to the copyright holders indicated in each case.

Every effort has been made to contact copyright holders of material reproduced in this book. Any omissions will be rectified in subsequent printings if notice is given to the publisher.

The manufacturer's authorised representative in the EU for product safety is Oxford University Press España S.A. of el Parque Empresarial San Fernando de Henares, Avenida de Castilla, 2–288 30 Madrid (www.oup.es/en).

Contents

In this book you will find stories, poems and facts from these places. We hope you enjoy them!

ARCTIC OCEAN

RUSSIA

ASIA

EUROPE

CHINA

JAPAN

BOTSWANA

INDIAN
OCEAN

OCEANIA

AUSTRALIA

UTHERN OCEAN

5

Unit contents

Unit	Theme	Country focus	Reading and comprehension
1	Young heroes	Alaska, USA	**Fiction** Kara's one big chance *White Dolphin* **Fiction** Going Hunting *Black Star, Bright Dawn* **Fiction** The Iditarod Great Sled Race *Black Star, Bright Dawn*
2	Health and sport	Oceans of the world, USA	**Non-fiction** Biography *Wilma Rudolph: Olympic athlete* **Non-fiction** Newspaper article *Gold! Gold! Gold!* **Non-fiction** Autobiography *Mike Perham: Sailing the Dream* **Non-fiction** Journalistic interview *We Salute You!*
3	Stormy weather	Italy, Worldwide	**Playscript** *The Tempest*
REVISE AND CHECK UNITS 1–3			
4	Traditional tales and fables	Tibet, Russia	**Fiction** *The Tiger and the Frog* **Fiction** *Peter and the Wolf (Part 1)* **Fiction** *Peter and the Wolf (Part 2)*
5	School days	Worldwide	**Non-fiction** *Welcome to our school family!* **Non-fiction** *Persuasive writing* **Non-fiction** *The pros and cons of homework*
6	Let's celebrate!	China, Australia	**Poetry** *Dragon Dance* **Poetry** *Celebration* **Poetry** *Sunbeam* **Poetry** *I love birthday parties!* **Poetry** *Tree Festival*
REVISE AND CHECK UNITS 4–6			
7	Spies and mystery	Africa, UK	**Fiction** Young Bond *Young Bond: Double or Die* **Fiction** How it all began *Stormbreaker* **Fiction** Alex becomes a spy *Stormbreaker* **Fiction** Botswana's greatest detective *Precious and the Monkeys: Precious Ramotswe's Very First Case*
8	Conserving our precious planet	Ecuador, Brazil, New Zealand	**Non-fiction** The Galápagos Islands *Expedition of a lifetime* **Non-fiction** Website report *Last chance for Māui dolphins* **Non-fiction** Information text *Conserving rainforests*
9	A treasure trove of poems	Egypt's Mediterranean coast, Worldwide	**Poetry** *The Tornado* **Poetry** *It's only the storm* **Poetry** Kennings *Historian and Who is this?* **Poetry** *My Dad's a Secret Agent*
REVISE AND CHECK UNITS 7–9			
POETRY READING *Adventures of Isabel* and *The 'Veggy' Lion*			

Unit	Language, grammar, spelling, vocabulary, phonics	Writing	Speaking and listening
1	• Sentence length and structure • Main and subordinate clauses • Direct speech • Colons and semicolons • Narrative voice and viewpoint	**Fiction** Narrative story structure	Organisation of ideas Expression of ideas
2	• Adverbials of time • Prefixes and suffixes • Single and multi-clause sentences	**Non-fiction** Writing an interview	Expression of ideas
3	• Modal verbs • Commas, dashes and brackets • Word origins	**Playscripts** Writing a playscript	Expressing opinions Performing a playscript
REVISE AND CHECK UNITS 1–3			
4	• Word classes • Shades of meaning • Adjectives • Adjectives and adverbs • The /k/ sound	**Fiction** Descriptive writing: Describing a forest Writing a modern folk tale	Spoken presentation Expressing opinions
5	• Persuasive language • Persuasive punctuation • Conjunctions, adverbs and adverbials • Relative clauses and relative pronouns	**Non-fiction** Writing to persuade	Expressing opinions Expression of ideas Speaking to persuade
6	• Tricky spellings • Difficult words and homophones • Figurative language	**Poetry** Writing a celebration poem	Expression and explanation of ideas Language choices Spoken presentation Poetry performance
REVISE AND CHECK UNITS 4–6			
7	• Narrative voice and viewpoint • Word origins • Proverbs and idioms • Active and passive voice	**Fiction** Writing an action thriller	Expressing opinions Reading a story aloud with expression
8	• Using imperative verbs • Adverbials of time • Multi-clause sentences • Quantifiers	**Non-fiction** Writing a non-chronological report	Organisation of ideas Expressing opinions
9	• Compound words • Speech marks • The /k/ sound, /ch/ sound and /j/ sound	**Poetry** Writing a kenning poem about being a spy	Expression of ideas Poetry performance
REVISE AND CHECK UNITS 7–9			
POETRY READING *Adventures of Isabel* and *The 'Veggy' Lion*			

Greta Thunberg

The Iditarod is a very challenging long-distance sled dog race held every March. The people driving the dog sleds, known as mushers, travel 1,600 km through harsh landscapes and difficult weather conditions. In a storm, the wind chill can be as low as −90°C. The race is the most popular sporting event in Alaska and successful mushers are national heroes.

"If you have no confidence in self you are twice defeated in the race of life. With confidence you have won even before you have started."

Marcus Garvey

Talk time

1 Greta Thunberg is famous for giving speeches about climate change while she was still a teenager. Are there any young people in your country who are famous for doing something amazing?

2 Have you worked together in a team to achieve a challenging goal?

3 List three advantages of working together as a team on a project.

- Discuss teamwork
- Learn about heroes
- Find word meanings using context
- Learn about proverbs

A You don't need to be famous to be a hero. You can be a hero by:

- taking care of your friends
- helping your family
- looking after the environment and getting others to join you.

Think of three more ways to be a hero.

B Look at these words and definitions. Use each one in a sentence of your own.

campaign work in an organised and active way towards a goal
a good cause something good to do because it is helping others
protest show that you don't agree with something or someone
worthy something good that deserves support

C Below are some sayings, or proverbs, used by the Inuit people of Alaska. Work in pairs to discuss their meanings. Do you have any similar sayings in your language?

- If you are going to walk on thin ice, you might as well dance.
- Unless you're the lead sled dog, the view is pretty much the same.
- You never really know your friends from your enemies until the ice breaks.
- The **caribou** feeds the wolf, but it is the wolf who keeps the caribou strong.

Glossary

caribou large North American deer

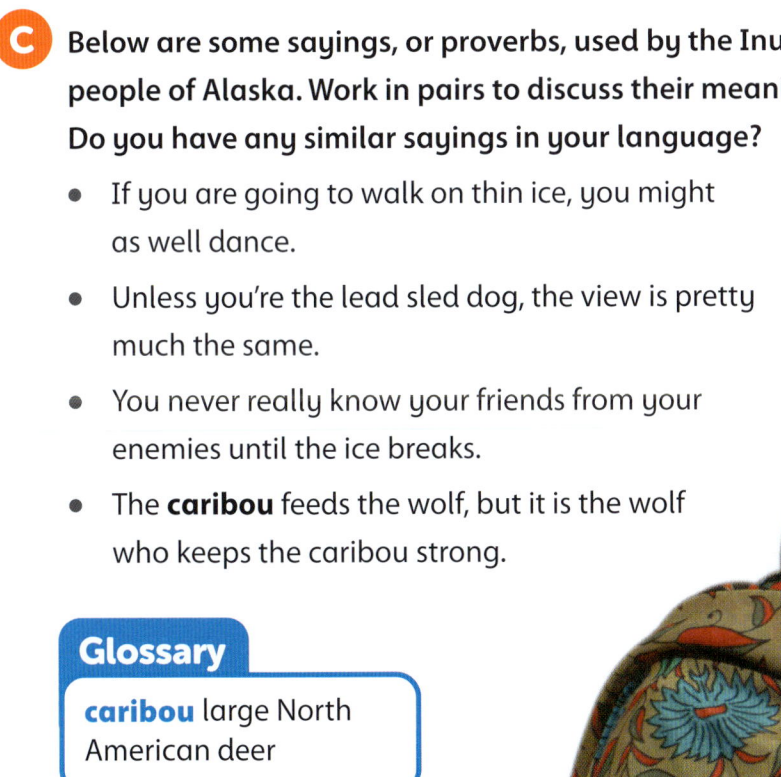

Malala Yousafzai won the Nobel Peace Prize for her campaign highlighting the need for girls in Pakistan to be allowed an education.

9

Reef at risk

Kara saves an injured dolphin, then starts a campaign to protect the nearby **reef** from damage by overfishing. Kara's mother made a film about the reef before she died. The film is shown to the public and Kara finds the **courage** to stand up in front of all the townspeople to say what she believes.

Kara's one big chance

The hall is silent, listening. "Fishing *is* the heart of this town." I look around. This is my one big chance.

"The boat my mum and dad rebuilt together, fished from this harbour a hundred years ago. Back then, she would have
5 come home so full the fish would have been spilling over her sides into the sea." I swallow hard. The back of my throat is dry. I look around and fix my eye on Dougie Evans. "But she can't do that anymore. We've taken all the fish from our seas. Dougie Evans's **trawlers** have to go further and deeper to
10 find fish, and even then they sometimes come back empty. Now we're tearing up the reef. I wonder, will we still be fishing here at all in another hundred years?" I glance across the hall. There's no sign of Felix, but I remember what he wanted me to say. "You're about to see what we could lose."

15 I stand there in the silence and look around the hall. I don't know what's meant to happen now. I climb down the steps and sit next to Dad.

The hall lights go out.

I hear Mum, speaking through the darkness.

20 The room is silent. The huge screen on the stage is dark at first. A faint greenish glow in the centre of the screen becomes brighter and brighter and we are rising up, towards the sun shining through the surface of the water. A seal
25 swims up to the camera. It's as if he's watching everyone in the hall. His big dog eyes are chocolate brown. Silver bubbles spiral upwards and he twists away, his grey body sliding through the water. And we're twisting through
30 the water too: down, down, down through rippling sunlight, past rocks jewelled with pink and green **anemones**, down past **coral** mounds and **sea-fans**.

Glossary

reef area under the sea which is made of rock, coral or sand

courage behave bravely

trawlers fishing boats

anemones sea creatures that look like flowers

coral colourful living creatures which grow into reefs after many years

sea-fans fan-shaped sea creatures

- Find information to answer questions
- Relate writing to wider issues

35 This must have been the last film mum made here in the bay...

But suddenly, a tearing sound rips through the hall. The image on the screen changes and fills with metal chains and **billowing** mud and sand. When the mud settles all that's left is a gravelly sea bed, littered with broken 40 sea-fans. The silence in the hall is still and deep.

Mum's voice speaks out one last time.

"Unless we protect our oceans, there will be nothing left but wasteland. We are not farmers of the sea. We never **sow**, we only **reap**."

45 The lights come on. No one speaks. A ripple of applause starts at the back of the room and rolls forward like a wave. I look across to see some of the fishermen nodding. Others are just staring at the screen, **transfixed**.

From *White Dolphin* by Gill Lewis

Glossary

billowing moving up and down in wind or water

sow plant, for example, by scattering seeds in soil

reap gather in a crop or harvest

transfixed focused very closely on something

Comprehension

A Listen and respond

1 How do we know Kara is nervous when she is giving her talk?

2 Why are there no fish left?

3 What are the fishermen destroying while they're fishing?

B Read and respond

1 Who or what does 'she' refer to on line 4?

2 How do we know the townspeople are impressed by Kara's presentation?

3 Which phrases in the text indicate that the sea bed is being damaged by fishing?

C What do you think?

What do you think will happen in the future if changes aren't made to the present fishing methods?

This reef has been damaged by a fisherman's anchor.

Sentence length in fiction texts

A In the extract from *White Dolphin* by Gill Lewis, the writer uses short sentences for dramatic effect. Look at the short sentences underlined below.

<u>The lights come on. No one speaks</u>. A ripple of applause starts at the back of the room and rolls forward like a wave. I look across to see some of the fishermen nodding. Others are just staring at the screen.

1 Join the first two sentences into one sentence, using 'and' to join them.

2 What is the effect of 'losing' the short sentences?

B Rewrite the text below and remove all 'ands' except for one. You'll find it is a better piece of writing with some effective short sentences.

Language tips
- When you use 'and', consider whether you need to start a new sentence instead.
- Vary sentence length in your writing, so that there are both long and short sentences.

It all started when I arrived home and I could see that the front door had been left open and I felt a bit frightened and I wondered whether someone had broken in, so I opened the door very carefully and I tiptoed in and at first I couldn't see anything and I breathed a huge sigh of relief and suddenly, I heard a scream and I wanted to run for my life, but I knew I had to investigate and slowly, I made my way to the living room and I opened the door very, very gently and I saw my mother with a broken television at her feet and she had bought a new television, brought it in herself and, as it was too heavy, had dropped it and she had been so busy struggling with all of this that she hadn't managed to close the door and there hadn't been a burglar after all!

C Write a short account of arriving at your house late at night.

Main and subordinate clauses

- Examine multi-clause sentences
- Look at participle verbs
- Change the position of clauses

A multi-clause sentence consists of a **main clause** and one or more **subordinate** clauses.

A subordinate clause cannot stand alone, and is usually introduced by a **subordinating conjunction** such as: when, where, if, although, since, until, as.

Examples: I like you **when you are in a good mood**. The library, **where I spend my free time,** is ten minutes away.

A Sometimes the subordinating conjunction is missed out.

Example: I can hear my brother **who** is moaning about the holiday to his friends.
Can be written as: I can hear my brother moaning about the holiday to his friends.

Rewrite the following sentences, missing out the subordinating conjunction.

1 I saw my friend <u>who was</u> running up the stairs.

2 The boy <u>who is</u> sitting in the office is waiting for his mother.

3 I'll put the money <u>that</u> I got from Nan towards a new game.

B Sometimes a present participle verb (ending in '–ing') or past participle verb (ending in '–ed') can come at the beginning of a sentence.

Examples: Smiling to himself, he started walking home.
Tired after a long day, she fell asleep immediately.

Write four sentences beginning each one with a different participle verb from the list below.

running   laughing   exhausted   frightened

C Subordinate clauses can be placed at different points in a sentence.

Examples: Although Kara spoke clearly, they didn't understand her.
They didn't understand her, although Kara spoke clearly.

Complete these sentences and put the clauses in different positions.

When I have free time, I...

She did her homework...

As soon as I got home from school...

Alaskan adventure (Part 1)

In Alaska, it is November and the sea has frozen over. A young Alaskan girl, Bright Dawn, and her father are waiting to go hunting. After waiting for over a week for narrow passages of open water, known as leads, to appear in the ice, Bright Dawn's father can wait no longer. He decides to go hunting over land on a sled instead of by water in his **kayak**.

Going Hunting

Bartok, my father, decided not to wait for the leads to open. He told me to get the dog sled and **harness** the dogs. He would hunt without a kayak.

"We'll hunt bearded seals on the ice," he said. Bearded seals
5 are heavy. They can weigh six hundred pounds. I harnessed our seven dogs to the sled and chose Black Star to lead the team. Bartok did not like him. When Black Star was a year old, my father decided that he would never make a good leader.

10 "He's **stubborn**," my father said. "You tell him something and he does something else."

"He's smart," I said, remembering the winter when we were coming home and, just on the other side of Salmon Creek, Black Star pulled up and wouldn't move. My father walked out on the frozen creek and fell through
15 the ice up to his neck. I remembered this time but said nothing about it. "Black Star knows a lot," I said.

"Of the wrong things," Bartok said. "He's got too much wolf in him. His father came from Baffin Bay and had a lot of wolf blood."

I liked Black Star. I had liked him since he was a month old. There were
20 seven in the **litter** and he was the most playful of them all. He bounced around and took nothing from his brothers and sisters, giving two bites back for every one he got.

He was the purest white, with a black star on his forehead and black slashes under big eyes. But of everything, it was his eyes themselves
25 that captured me. They were ice-blue. At first I thought how cold and **suspicious** and wild they were, looking at me from a world I had never seen and would never know.

Glossary

kayak small canoe or boat

harness add straps so you can control something

stubborn fixed in opinion or behaviour

litter animals born at the same time to the same mother

suspicious not trusting

- Find information to answer questions
- Make inferences about a character
- Write a character profile

After a while, I felt that behind this was a shadow of friendship. That changed and I saw nothing but
30 friendliness. Then that changed, too.

Sometimes, when moon shadows were on the trail and we were hunting things down from the forest, the wild look would come back again.

From *Black Star, Bright Dawn* by Scott O'Dell

Comprehension

A   **Read and respond**

1   Whose point of view is the story told from?

2   Why did Bartok decide to hunt by sled?

3   Why would a sled be needed to hunt bearded seals?

4   Why did Bartok believe that Black Star would never make a good team leader?

5   What does Bright Dawn say is Black Star's most remarkable feature?

6   Explain how Bright Dawn's opinion of Black Star changed over time.

B   **What do you think?**
Discuss these questions with your partner then write answers using evidence from the extract to help you.

1   Why did Bright Dawn choose not to remind her father what had happened near Salmon Creek?

2   Do you think Black Star can make a good team leader? Why/Why not?

3   Why does Black Star sometimes have a 'wild look'?

C   **Discuss**
With a partner, discuss everything you know about Black Star. What do you know about his appearance and character? What can you guess about his appearance or character using evidence from the extract to help you?

Direct speech

When you use **direct speech** in your own stories, check that the punctuation is correct. Also, remember that for each new speaker, the text needs to start on a new line.

Examples: "He's stubborn," my father said. "You tell him something and he does something else."

"He's smart," I said, remembering the winter when we were coming home... "Black Star knows a lot," I said.

"Of the wrong things," Bartok said.

Sometimes, try to use more precise verbs than 'said.'

Examples: muttered, shouted, argued, whispered

You could even add adverbs.

Examples: loudly, quietly

A Rewrite the dialogue below, starting new lines for new speakers. Replace 'said' with other verbs. Perhaps add some adverbs too.

"I want to go sledding," said Aputi. "I can't stand staying indoors all day." "I thought you had homework to do," said Mum. "Oh, Mum," said Aputi. "I've almost finished it. Can't I just take an hour off?" "Yes," said Mum, "but only when you've finished your work." "But it'll be dark if I don't go soon!" said Aputi. "Then you'd better hurry up and finish your homework," said Mum.

B Rewrite the following dialogue, inserting correct punctuation and starting new lines for new speakers.

Excuse me, said the man. Can you tell me what time it is? I seem to have left my watch at home. He chuckled. I am becoming very forgetful in my old age! I think it's about 8 o'clock said Anuk laughing. I actually haven't got my watch on, but I do remember seeing the time on the town hall clock. The town hall! said the man. That's just the place I'm looking for. Can you point me in the right direction? Certainly Anuk said.

C Write a short conversation between two people. When you are finished, give your writing to a partner so they can check that you have used the correct punctuation.

Colons and semicolons

- Learn about colons and semicolons
- Use them correctly

A **colon :** is used to begin a list.

Example: In her pencil case, Jana has: a ruler, an eraser, scissors, pencils and a pencil sharpener.

A Write the sentences out, putting the colons in the correct places.

1 I have lived in many cities Rome, Sydney, Dubai and London.

2 Your plan has three advantages it is cheap, it is sensible and it is fun.

3 Roald Dahl writes children's books, short stories, novels and poems.

A **semicolon ;** can be used to separate longer phrases in a list.

Commas are already used within the short phrases, so using a semicolon makes the list of items clearer.

Example: Yesterday, I bought these items: some large, ripe bananas; six large, fresh bread rolls; a small, blue bowl; and three boxes of tea.

B Write a sentence listing the items from Bright Dawn's sled. Use a colon before the list starts and semicolons in between the items.

a pair of walking boots	half a chocolate bar	a first aid kit
a sleeping bag	fur-lined slippers	a bottle of water

A **semicolon** can also be used instead of **and** or **but** to join two related sentences.

Example: The boy burst through the door **and** he glared at me.
The boy burst through the door**;** he glared at me.

C Match the sentences below using a semicolon to join them.

Example: Fruit is good for you; burgers are not.

I listened to the rain	he prefers tennis.
The plates are in the cupboard	I love rain.
She loves playing football	the spoons are in the drawer.

Alaskan adventure (Part 2)

Bright Dawn's father becomes sick. For the honour of the village, she must take her father's place in a difficult sled dog race that covers 1,600 kilometres. Running with ears laid back and nose in the air, Black Star, leader of her dog team, guides them through dangers on the race trail.

The Iditarod Great Sled Race

The country beyond looked wild and <u>forsaken</u>. Scattered trees were **ragged** and bent over by fierce winds. It was very cold.

I drove the team faster than I ever had before. At times we were running at fifteen miles an hour. The dogs opened
5 their jaws and <u>scooped</u> up snow as they ran…

The trail wound through steep hills and the temperature was now much below zero. My eyelashes gathered frost and began to feel like **splinters**. I had a hard time seeing and had to depend on Black Star.

10 I was travelling on a **lagoon** formed by the Innoko River when the trail began to tremble. At once I realized that we were on ice, thin ice, no more than a couple of inches thick. Ahead of us it was <u>billowing</u> like waves on the sea.

Black Star saw the billows too and stopped the dogs. If
15 we went on, the whole team, all of us, would go crashing down into the rushing river. We were trapped. Panic <u>seized</u> me. Black Star stood with his ears curled back tight against his head. He was trying to decide where to go, to the right or to the left. I was of no help. It was Black Star's decision.

20 At last he turned toward a line of trees that marked the **shore**. He went slowly and the team followed him.

The ice grew thinner. It creaked beneath the weight of the sled. Through the ice I could see fish swimming and blue water racing over the rocks. Black Star's head was up and his
25 ears alert, his bushy tail curved high over his back. The rest of the team were dragging their tails. Suddenly Black Star pulled up. Then, slowly gathering speed, with the **bank** only a few yards away, he made a dash and scrambled safely to shore.

Glossary

ragged torn and broken-looking

splinters small, sharp pieces of wood or glass

lagoon area of salt water separated from the sea

shore/bank land along the edge of some water

handlebar the steering bar of something like a bike or sled

current water or air moving strongly in a definite direction

towline line or rope used to pull something

The next five dogs followed him. Then the ice broke and the
30 rest of the team fell through into the swirling water. The sled
went with them and I went with the sled.

Dazed and blinded, I held tight to the sled **handlebar**.
The dogs were struggling against the **current**, their heads up
and silent. There was a gray mist among the trees, but I had a
35 glimpse of my leader. He and his five dogs were pulling on the
towline. With all my strength I shouted, "Go, Black Star, go!"

From *Black Star, Bright Dawn* by Scott O'Dell

Comprehension

A Listen and respond

1 How fast were Bright Dawn and her dogs travelling?

2 Why did Bright Dawn have to depend on Black Star to lead
the way?

3 What made Bright Dawn first realise she was on thin ice?

B Read and respond

1 Why does Black Star pull the sled to a standstill?

2 Number these statements 1–3 so that they are in the right order.

- Black Star and five dogs make it to the shore.
- Bright Dawn and some dogs crash through the ice.
- Bright Dawn and the dog team are travelling very fast.

3 Bright Dawn believes Black Star is in control. Find two pieces
of evidence from the extract which shows us this.

4 When the team is in danger, what is it about Black Star that
shows he is more alert than the other dogs?

5 Match the underlined words from the extract to the correct
meanings below.

Use the context of the extract to help you decide.

- pick up something in a quick, smooth movement
- abandoned, nothing there
- took hold of something suddenly and strongly
- a quick look at something
- moving up and down in the breeze
- reaction to shock, unable to think or act properly

● Learn how language can increase tension

C **What do you think?**

Work with a partner to discuss the answers to these questions.

1 Find three phrases which show the race takes place in harsh conditions.

2 Find some examples of short sentences in the extract. What mood does this create?

3 Choose six verbs from the extract to show the writer has created a mood of tension and movement.

4 How are Black Star and the five dogs who made it on land going to save Bright Dawn and the other dogs? Complete the story with your partner.

The person in charge of the dog sled is called a musher or driver.

First person narrative

The extracts *Kara's one big chance* and *The Iditarod Great Sled Race* are both **first person narratives**. They are written from the point of view of the main character and not an outside-the-story narrator. Look at the main features of first person narratives below and find examples of these features in the extracts.

- Use pronouns 'I' and 'we'.
- The reader knows what the main character is thinking and feeling.
- The reader sees everything from the main character's point of view.
- The reader only knows what the main character knows and shares with them.
- The reader doesn't know what other characters are thinking or feeling.

A **1** Look at the event described below from an onlooker's viewpoint.

> The older boy crept up behind the girl, a mean smile on his face. It was obvious they were brother and sister because they shared the same black curls and olive skin. The boy suddenly reached over and grabbed his sister's ball. He kicked it far away across the park, then laughed and ran off. His sister stood and stared at him with her angry dark eyes, trying hard not to cry.

2 Rewrite the event from the point of view of the girl or the boy.

B How is a story told from the main character's point of view different to a story told by an outside-the-story narrator? Think about the following:

- the characters' appearances
- the characters' thoughts and feelings
- how the events are described.

C With a partner, retell the story from Black Star's point of view – as if he is telling the story – describing the great rescue with lots of excitement and tension.

- Look at first person narrative
- Revise narrative structure

Fiction writing workshop

Narrative structure

All stories have a similar structure.

- The **introduction** of **setting** and **main characters** tells us when and where the story happens and to whom.
- The **build-up** of the **setting** and **main characters** in the story – where we learn more about the setting and characters.
- The introduction of the **problem**, making us want to read on to find out what happens next.
- The build-up of the **problem**, where the situation gets worse and worse and tension is built up.
- The **climax** is the most exciting point when something terrible or wonderful happens.
- The **resolution** is how the problem is fixed and explains how the story ends.

Model writing

Read the extract on pages 18–19 again. Copy and complete the narrative structure table below using examples from the extract. Use your own ending of the story from activity C on page 20 as the resolution.

The **introduction** of **setting** and **main characters**	Alaska, Bright Dawn and Black Star
The **build-up** of the **setting** and **main characters**	
The introduction of the **problem**	
The build-up of the **problem**	
The **climax**	
The **resolution**	

Writing a first person narrative story

- Use a table for notes and structure
- Write a first person narrative
- Use sentence length and language for effect

Write a short story called *Danger in the Wilderness* where you are the main character. Choose one of the scenarios below.

1. You (+ one other – human or animal) are on a snowmobile in the Alaskan wilderness when you suddenly meet a polar bear.
2. You (+ one other) are in a kayak on a river in the middle of the Amazon jungle when you see the river ahead is about to get very dangerous.
3. You (+ one other) are on a camping trip, deep in the woods when you hear the sound of something very big moving nearby.
4. Your own ideas.

Planning your narrative

Plan your story by copying and completing the table below with your ideas. (Just write the important words or phrases.) Think of an exciting opening to grab the readers' attention. Write some powerful adjectives and adverbs you can use to describe the setting and characters. Include powerful verbs to keep the action exciting. Add similes or metaphors to help the reader imagine the danger. For the ending, you could leave your story on an exciting cliffhanger, so the reader has to guess what happens next!

The **introduction** of **setting** and **main characters**	
The **build-up** of the **setting** and **main characters**	
The introduction of the **problem**	
The build-up of the **problem**	
The **climax**	
The **resolution**	

23

Talking through your narrative

Use your plan to tell your story to your partner. Listen carefully to your partner's story. Are the setting and main characters described well? Does the story build up to an exciting climax? Do the events follow on from each other logically and make complete sense? Is there a satisfactory ending? Give each other feedback. Say what you think works really well and what can be done to make the story even better.

Using powerful language

Think about whether you could use more powerful language in your story, such as similes, metaphors or personification. Could you use more powerful verbs? Complete the activity below to help you understand how you could edit your work to make your writing more powerful.

1   Look at the description below. Use figurative language such as simile, metaphors or personification to transform the underlined sentences.

   Example: Instead of 'The moon shone in the black sky.' You could write: The pale moon shone a beam of silver torchlight across the black sky.

   The moon shone in the black sky. The dark clouds moved quickly in the wind. I walked through the forest, the trees shaking as the icy wind blew their branches. I felt cold. Suddenly, I saw a huge, dark shadow moving towards me. I hid behind a tree trunk. It moved slowly towards me. It stopped, put its head right back and shouted. It was a scary sound. Then it turned and walked away from me.

2   Identify six verbs and swap them for more powerful verbs. *Example:* walked – trudged.

3   Now return to your own story and see what improvements you could make to the language.

Writing your narrative

- Use feedback to write a final draft
- Proofread your final draft

Use your notes, your partner's feedback and the success criteria below to write your story. When you have finished, reread what you have written and edit it carefully. Check that your events follow on logically from each other and that you have used the correct punctuation, grammar and spelling. If you have time, look up any words you are unsure of in a dictionary. When ready, swap your story with a new partner. Use the success criteria to give each other feedback.

Language tip

Remember to use short sentences to build tension.

First person narrative success criteria

First person point of view is consistent throughout, using pronouns 'I' and 'we'.

The setting is well-described (using powerful verbs and adjectives to add interest).

The characters are well-described (using powerful adjectives and adverbs to add interest).

Powerful verbs are used to create exciting action.

A mixture of short and long sentences are used to build up tension.

The action builds up to an exciting climax.

The past tense is used consistently throughout the story.

The correct spelling, punctuation and grammar is used throughout the story.

There is a satisfactory resolution – the story ends on an exciting cliffhanger or the problem is solved.

2 Health and sport

Sachin Tendulkar batting for India

Saudi women's team

New Zealand player Lydia Ko, aged 15

Fiji playing against Samoa

"Obstacles don't have to stop you. If you run into a wall, don't turn around and give up. Figure out how to climb it, go through it, or work around it."

Michael Jordan

Talk time

1 Name the sport in each picture.

2 What are the most popular sports in your country?

3 Do you enjoy sports? Which sports do you enjoy most? Why? Which sports do you not enjoy? Why?

- Express your ideas
- Have a discussion
- Explain the results of a quiz

Are you fit and healthy?

Exercise Quiz

1 How often do you do sports at school?

   a twice a week or less

   b more than twice a week

   c every day

2 In your free time, how often do you do physical exercise?

   a never

   b twice a week or less

   c more than twice a week

3 If someone is playing sports at break, how often do you join in?

   a never

   b sometimes

   c always

4 There's a sports day in your school. Do you usually:

   a not take part

   b sign up for your favourite and best event

   c sign up for all the events?

Compare your answers with your partner and check your score using the answer key.

Answer key

a answers = 1 point each **b** answers = 3 points each

c answers = 5 points each

Over 15 points: Well done! You are really fit!

Over 10 points: You are on the right road. Keep going!

Less than 10 points: Exercise is good for you. Try to do a little more if you can.

 Stretch zone

Write about a sport that you have taken part in or watched.

● Read about an inspiring person

A biography of Wilma Rudolph: Olympic athlete

Introduction

Wilma Rudolph won three gold medals at the Olympic Games in Rome in 1960. Wilma was the first American woman to achieve such success.

Early years

Wilma was born **prematurely** in Tennessee, USA in June 1940. Because she was born early, Wilma was often ill. One illness – Polio – was so bad that Wilma had to wear a **brace** on her leg. Doctors told Wilma's mother that Wilma probably wouldn't walk again. However, with determination and the help of **physical therapy**, Wilma recovered. By the age of 11, Wilma was very interested in sport – particularly basketball.

The Olympics

During her time at high school, Wilma got a place at the 1956 Olympic Games in Melbourne, Australia. Wilma was only 16 when she became the youngest member of the American Olympic team. Wilma's team won a bronze medal for the **sprint relay.**

After that, Wilma studied at Tennessee State University. Here, Wilma met her future coach – Ed Temple – who helped her improve as an athlete and win even more awards.

Next, Wilma went to the 1960 Rome Olympic Games. Wilma became the first American woman – black or white – to win three Olympic gold medals in one games. Wilma won the 100m, the 200m and the 4×100m relay. As well as this, Wilma set new world record times in each event.

Wilma became famous around the world. In 1960 and 1961, Wilma was awarded the title of Associated Press Woman Athlete of the Year.

Glossary

prematurely too early
brace metal device giving support
physical therapy movements and exercises to help someone get better
sprint relay team of runners run part of the race each
retired stopped work
equality being treated the same as everyone else

leg brace

- Find information to answer questions
- Look at key features of a biography

Later years

Wilma **retired** in the early 1960s and became a teacher and a sports coach. She married Robert Eldridge in 1963 and the couple had four children. Wilma died of cancer on 12 November 1994, aged just 54.

Conclusion

Wilma is remembered as being one of the fastest women on the athletics track and a powerful voice for African Americans and **equality**.

What did you find most interesting about Wilma's life? Do you think we can learn from famous sports people? What can we learn from Wilma?

Comprehension

A **Listen and respond**

1 What is Wilma most famous for?

2 Why is it surprising that Wilma became a good runner?

3 Who did Wilma meet at university? How did he help her?

B **Read and respond**

1 What is the purpose of a biography?

2 Find evidence of these biography features in the extract.

- Important dates follow in chronological order
- Written in the past tense
- Written in the third person / an impersonal style

C **What do you think?**

1 Research a famous sports person from history. Make notes on them using the following subheadings:

Introduction (who they are and why are they famous)

Early years (where they were born, family, childhood)

Big sporting events (which events they were famous for)

Later years (what they did after they stopped playing sport)

Conclusion (how they are remembered, what you think of them, what qualities they had which made them succeed)

2 Use your notes to write a full biography of your chosen sports person.

Adverbials of time

Look at the following short biography of Mae Faggs Starr, one of Wilma Rudolph's team mates. **Adverbials of time** (**in bold**) have been used to show the order of events in her life. Adverbials of time are very helpful if you want to show *when* something happens, especially if it happens in a certain order.

Example: **First**, Mae went to the 1952 Olympics in Finland, where her team won a gold medal for their sprint relay. **Next**, Mae won the USA Outdoor Track and Field Championships in the 100-yard dash in 1955. **After that**, Mae and Wilma won bronze at the 1956 Olympics in Australia for their sprint relay. **Later**, Mae taught athletics in a high school.

 1 Reread the biography of Wilma Rudolph on page 28 and find two adverbials of time.

2 Imagine that someone is writing a biography about you. What would you want people to know? Think about the important events in your life so far, and also your best qualities.

3 Write your own short biography using third person narrative and adverbials of time.

4 Now imagine someone is writing a biography about you in ten years' time. What sort of a person would you like to become?

● Use adverbials of time in sequencing

B **Adverbials of time are useful for giving clear instructions for how to do something.**

● Using the words below, write a list of adverbials of time that you would use at the **start** of instructions.

● Then write a list of adverbials of time that you would use in the **middle** of instructions.

● Then write a list of adverbials of time that you would use at the **end** of instructions.

> eventually   first of all   firstly   secondly   lastly
> then   next   after that   to begin with   finally   first

C **1** Now use your adverbials of time to write instructions for how to get ready to play a sport. For example, for a game of tennis:

First, find a partner to play with and **then** find some rackets and a ball. **Next**, set up the net across your tennis court. **After that**, decide who will play on which side of the court.

Lastly, do a quick warm-up to stretch your muscles. **Finally**, start to play by hitting the ball to your partner.

2 Try swapping your adverbials of time for others in your lists.

- Learn more about an inspiring person

Newspaper article

Here is an article about Wilma Rudolph from a newspaper in 1960.

Gold! Gold! Gold!

American athlete Wilma Rudolph made history today by winning a third Olympic gold medal in Rome.

A triple winner

Wilma was part of the American team in the 4×100m **relay**. They recorded a winning time of 44.5 seconds.

20-year-old Rudolph was also **victorious** in the 200m final.

There was concern about Rudolph's fitness to run the 100m final because she'd twisted her ankle the day before. But, in spite of her injury, Rudolph still went on to win. She will surely be proud of becoming the first American woman in history to win three gold medals at a single Olympic Games.

Record breaking

As well as her three medals, Rudolph broke several world records. Her relay team set a record-breaking time of 44.4 seconds in the 100m relay semi-finals. Rudolph also set another record of 23.2 seconds in the opening race of the 200m dash. Even her 100m final time of 11.0 seconds would have been a world record, but due to a technical issue it wasn't allowed.

An electric atmosphere

Thousands of people watched the relay event. One eye witness described it: "It was amazing. The atmosphere was electric." It was very tense as the US team were in second place. They were nearly 2 metres behind after a poor **baton** pass, but Rudolph was determined and soon closed the gap. Rudolph went on to win by more than 2.5 metres.

Rudolph's historic achievement has brought her international respect in Rome and she no doubt will return home a national hero.

The three winners of the women's 100m final in Rome.

Glossary

relay team of runners who each run part of the race

victorious having won

baton stick which is passed from person to person in a relay race

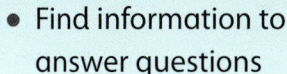

- Find information to answer questions
- Look at key features of a newspaper report

Comprehension

A **Listen and respond**

1 Where were the 1960 Olympics held?

2 What did Wilma do the day before the final of the 100m race?

3 What was Wilma the first American woman to do?

B **Read and respond**

1 What was the world record time set by Wilma for the 200m dash?

2 Why was Wilma's record time of 11 seconds not accepted in the final?

3 How many metres did Wilma win by in the relay event?

C **What do you think?**

Discuss these questions with your partner.
Use the information in the article to help you.

1 Look at the headline. What figurative technique is used? Is the headline effective? Can you think of a more effective headline?

2 Look at the following phrases from the article. Explain what they mean:
- made history today
- break a world record
- electric atmosphere
- an eye witness

3 What does Wilma Rudolph's achievement teach us?

 **Stretch zone**

Write about someone you think is inspirational. Explain why you admire them and how they inspire others.

- Read about another inspirational person

Autobiography

In August 2009, Mike Perham sailed around the world on his own. He was only 17 years, 5 months and 11 days old. He therefore became the youngest person to sail solo around the world. His book, *Sailing the Dream*, is his autobiography. It tells the story of his amazing voyage. Here is an extract from the book.

Sailing the Dream

Midnight. The boat flew over the Southern Ocean in the darkness. Everything inside rattled and shook as she surfed the waves. The speed! It was amazing. Twenty-six **knots** on my boat was just insane.

5   Not for one moment did I wish I was on dry land. I was scared, for sure, but not panicked. Panic is not something I normally associate with the ocean. It's where I feel most at home. Its uncontrollable dangers are part of the life of a sailor like me.

10   I **wedged** myself inside the cabin, at the chart table, which was the safest place to be. I tried to work on the chart. It gave me something to do instead of just worrying about the conditions, which were **forecast** to continue for at least another twenty-four hours. Everything else was soaking wet

15   but I was okay.

The **freak** wave that came thundering through the darkness must have been enormous. Hiding away in the cabin, I didn't see it coming but I had a one-minute warning. Its **deafening** roar! It scooped the boat up and **slammed** it

20   flat on its side in an instant. Helpless, all I could do was hold my breath and **somersault** with the boat. The fear that hit me was instant. The noise was ridiculous; the boat creaked, groaned, rattled and screamed.

From *Sailing the Dream* by Mike Perham

Glossary

knots measurement of speed

wedged forced into a narrow space

forecast predicted

freak unusual

deafening loud

slammed thrown down with force

somersault flip over

- Find information to answer questions
- Compare biographies and autobiographies
- Write an account

Comprehension

A **Read and respond**

1 Which verb in the first paragraph of *Sailing the Dream* shows how quickly the boat is moving?

2 Which word from the list below best describes the writer's mood in the first paragraph? Give evidence from the extract to support your answer.

> frightened   excited   bored   sad

3 Which one of the following statements is true about the writer?

- He usually feels comfortable on the ocean.
- He believes it is safe on the water.
- He isn't worried about the weather conditions.

4 What does the writer do to try to keep himself calm?

B **What do you think?**

Discuss these questions with your partner.

1 Do you agree that the writer doesn't panic? Find evidence in the extract to support your answer.

2 How does the writer know that a huge wave is about to hit the boat?

3 In the last paragraph, does the writer feel in control? Which word shows this?

4 Does the extract contain fact, opinions, or both? Can you give examples?

C **What about you?**

Think of an exciting event in your life, like a sports event. Use the plan below to write about what happened.

Paragraph 1

Set the scene – describe what you could hear, smell and touch. How did you feel?

Paragraph 2

What happened next? Why was it so exciting?

You could use short sentences to make it sound dramatic, and lots of adjectives to describe it in detail.

Paragraph 3

What happened at the end?

You could leave the ending open, like the extract, or finish the story.

• Learn about prefixes and suffixes

Prefixes and suffixes

A **prefix** is a group of letters added to the beginning of a word to change the meaning.
Examples: **pre-** means 'before'. So pre- + historic (prehistoric) means 'before history'.
im- means 'not'. So im- + possible (impossible) means 'not possible'.

A **1** Can you think of any more words that use the prefixes **pre-** and **im-**? You could use a dictionary to help you.

2 Some of the words in the extract from Mike Perham's book *Sailing the Dream* contain prefixes. Find words in the extract that use these prefixes. There is one word for each prefix.

Prefix	Meaning
in	not
un	not
fore	in front of

A **suffix** is a group of letters added to the end of a word to change the meaning.
Example: **-less** means 'without'. So wire + -less (wireless) means 'without wires'.

B Which three words below can have -less added to the end of them? Use a dictionary to help you.

hope   breed   fact   sleep   harm

C Write two words that end with the suffixes -able/-ible: able or fit to do something.

- Spell words ending /shun/
- Learn about suffixes -ance and -ence

More suffixes

Words that end in **-tion**, **-cian**, **-ssion** all make the same /shun/ sound, in spite of their different spellings.

We add **-cian** to a base word to describe a person who works in a certain job.
Example: diet – dietician

We use **-tion** when the base word ends with the 't' sound.
Example: educate – education

We use **-ssion** when the base word ends with -ss.
Example: progress – progression

A Complete these words ending with the /shun/ sound with one of the following endings. If you are not sure, use a dictionary to help you.

> -cian   -ssion   -tion

musi_____   direc_____   posse_____   correc_____

B Here are the definitions and root words of some words which end with the /shun/ sound. Write down the words which are being described.

1 A person who fixes electrical things. (electric)

2 A place. (locate)

3 Another word for an informal debate. (discuss)

-ance or **-ence**
An adjective ending in -ant can change to make a noun ending in **-ance**.
Examples: brilliant – brilliance   tolerant – tolerance
An adjective ending in -ent can change to make a noun ending in **-ence**.
Examples: different – difference   magnificent – magnificence

C Form the correct noun from the adjectives.

absent _____   significant _____

dominant _____   silent _____

Wheelchair athlete

◀ ▶ ↻ 🏠

We Salute You!

Aaron Fotheringham is a wheelchair athlete. Aaron is known as 'Wheelz', and is a **pioneer** in the sport of wheelchair motocross (WCMX). Aaron performs tricks and **stunts** in his wheelchair all over the world. At the age of 14, Aaron performed the first ever backflip in a wheelchair.

Aaron was born on 8 November 1991 in Las Vegas, Nevada, USA. Aaron has a **birth defect** called spina bifida which affects his **spine**.

What is wheelchair motocross?

WCMX is a term that I thought up for extreme wheelchairing in skateparks. It's **adapting** existing skateboard and BMX (bicycle motocross) moves for a wheelchair and making up new moves only a wheelchair can do.

When did you start this extreme sport?

My older brother, Brian, used to BMX and so he inspired me to start riding in skateparks. That was back in 2000.

How does it make you feel?

It makes me feel like I'm alive and not just playing video games.

What do you find hard?

Coming up with new tricks is the hardest thing I've found. And then after you come up with the trick, you actually have to land it!

How much time do you spend practising during each session?

It depends on the weather, but it can range from 2 to 8 hours.

What is your favourite trick?

The handplant. This is where you go up the quarter pipe (a curved, sloped ramp) and stall (balance) on one hand.

How did you feel when you did your first record-breaking backflip?

I was speechless! It was amazing. After all my hard work, I got my reward.

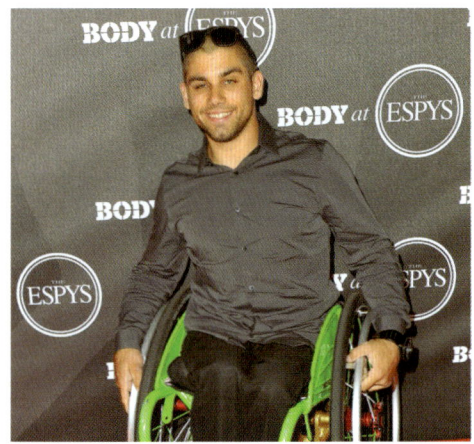

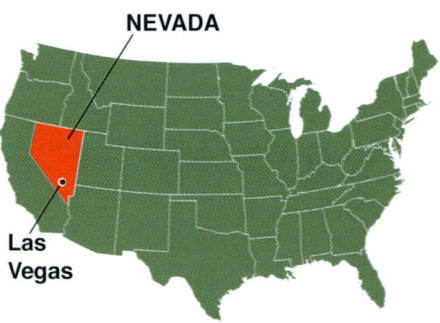

NEVADA

Las Vegas

Glossary

pioneer the first to do something

stunts exciting or dangerous actions

birth defect a problem that a baby is born with

spine line of bones down the middle of your back

adapting changing for a different purpose

- Find information to answer questions
- Identify key features of a magazine interview
- Write 'fact' and 'feeling' questions

Are there any tricks that you haven't been able to do yet?

It's not that I'm not able, it's just that I can't find a big enough ramp to be able to do them on!

Where would you like to see your sport go in the future?

I want to see it as a **category** in the X Games competition.

Comprehension

A Listen and respond

1 What is Aaron's nickname (a fun name given to someone instead of their real name)?

2 How old was Aaron when he did a stunt no one had managed before?

B Read and respond

1 Interviewers need to use the right type of question words. Identify three different 'wh' question words in the extract and write three more of your own.

2 Sometimes interviewers ask 'fact' questions and sometimes they ask 'feeling' questions. Write down one 'fact' question and one 'feeling' question from the extract.

3 Discuss with your partner which type of questions help the reader to understand the sport. Which type of questions help the reader to understand the sports person?

C What do you think?

1 With a partner, discuss four more questions that you could ask Aaron. Test your questions on each other. One of you can be the interviewer and the other can be Aaron.

2 Tell your partner which sports person you would like to interview.

3 Think of some questions you would like to ask your chosen sports person, then share them with your partner.

> **Glossary**
>
> **category** group of things which are the same or similar

> **?**
>
> You have read about Wilma Rudolph, Mike Perham and Aaron Fotheringham. Which of the three impressed you the most? Use information from the extracts to explain your answers. Do you think you could overcome the challenges these sports people faced? Has your idea of 'success' changed? What does success mean to you now?

- Learn about single and multi-clause sentences

Single and multi-clause sentences

Writers can choose from different types of sentences. A **single-clause sentence** has one subject and one verb.

Example: Aaron Fotheringham is a wheelchair athlete.

A **Find the verbs in each of these single-clause sentences.**

- Aaron holds a world record.
- My brother inspired me.
- I was speechless.
- He performed a backflip.

Writers can use **multi-clause sentences** to add more information or extra detail. Sometimes two single-clause sentences are joined by a **conjunction** such as 'and', 'but' or 'or'. Each clause contains a verb.

Example: Aaron Fotheringham holds a world record and he performed the first wheelchair backflip.

Some sentences have a **main clause** (which could stand alone as a sentence) and at least one **subordinate clause** (which provides more information).

Example: Aaron has been in a wheelchair since he was eight, because of his spina bifida.

B **1** Find two examples of sentences with two main clauses in the interview on page 38.

    2 Find two examples of sentences with a main and subordinate clause in the interview on page 38.

C **Write six sentences describing your favourite sport activity.**

    1 Write two single-clause sentences.

    2 Write two sentences with two main clauses.

    3 Write two sentences with a main and subordinate clause.

Fact or opinion?

A **fact** is something that can be proved to be correct.
Example: Aaron was born on 8 November 1991.

An **opinion** is what someone thinks or believes
Example: Aaron performs amazing stunts in his wheelchair.

Sometimes opinion can be made to sound like fact. Look at these two examples:

Aaron won the competition because he performed the highest jump. (Fact that can be proven.)

Aaron won the competition because he trained so hard. (An opinion – it can't be proven that training hard made him win.)

Read this extract from a news report.

Wheelz of steel!

Aaron Fotheringham, known as Wheelz to his fans, is a pioneer of freestyle wheelchair. Wheelz exploded onto the scene in 2006 after landing the first ever backflip on a wheelchair and he hasn't looked back since. He has broken several records and is the inspiration of millions of adults and kids. He performs on mega ramps and skateparks around the world, is completely fearless and is having the time of his life!

A Discuss with your partner which information is fact and which is opinion.

B Using the information in the extract, complete the following.
- Write six facts about Aaron.
- Write four opinions about Aaron.

C Write a paragraph about someone you know – a friend or family member. Include facts and opinions. Swap your paragraph with your partner. Can they identify which parts are facts and which are opinions?

Writing an article for a sports magazine

- Compare magazine articles and newspaper reports
- Write open and closed questions

A 'We Salute You!' is an article written for a BMX magazine (extreme bike sports). With your partner, compare 'We Salute You!' to the newspaper article on page 32. What do they have in common? What is different? What are the main features of the magazine article?

Journalists prepare their questions carefully to get the answers they want. There are two main types of question.

A **closed question** only needs a yes/no response or short answer.
Examples: Do you play doubles tennis? Yes.
What is the name of your doubles partner?
Naomi Osaka.

An **open question** encourages the interviewee to give more information.

Examples: Tell me about a typical day during a tennis tournament.
What were your reasons for pulling out of Wimbledon?

B Imagine that you work for a sports magazine and are going to write an article about a sports person you really admire.

What information do you think the readers would like to know? What would be an interesting topic that would make your readers want to read on?

C With your partner, write some questions that you would ask.

Examples:

How did you feel when you missed the…?

What was going through your head when…?

What is your greatest….?

Your writing

1 Now you are going to write the article. Use the plan below to help structure your notes. You may need to add a glossary if you use technical vocabulary. Remember to add a photograph and caption too.

Plan	Your notes
Headline – usually only 3–5 words long. You want to attract the interest of the reader by telling them what the article is about, in a short and interesting way.	
Opening paragraph – this sets the scene and summarises the sports person's life: date and place of birth, major childhood events, sporting achievements.	
Main body – this is the question and answer section. Questions should be open and in chronological order. Write 4–6 questions. Start with how and when the sports person became interested in the sport, then ask about achievements and what the sports person is doing currently. Finish on what they want to do in the future.	

2 Write your questions down, leaving enough room for answers beneath. Choose a partner and ask them to research your sports person. Then interview them in role as the sports person and write down their answers.

3 Use your notes and your partner's answers to write your article. When you have finished, reread it and edit your work to check if there are any spelling, punctuation or grammar mistakes.

4 Swap your article with a new partner. Use the list of success criteria below to give each other constructive feedback.
- Is the headline interesting?
- Is the opening paragraph short, with a few facts?
- Does the opening paragraph make you want to read on to find out more about the sports person?
- Are the questions grammatically correct?
- Do the questions encourage the interviewee to give lots of interesting information?
- Does the last question focus on the future?

5 Share your interviews with the class.

3 Stormy weather

1

2

3

> "Sunshine is delicious, rain is refreshing, wind braces us up, snow is exhilarating; there is really no such thing as bad weather, only different kinds of good weather."
> John Ruskin

Talk time

Look at the examples of stormy weather in the pictures.

1 What weather events do these pictures show?

2 What extreme weather or events have happened in your country? Explain them to a partner.

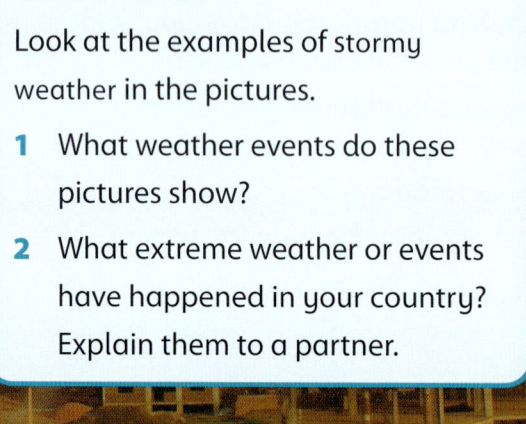

Extreme events

- Express ideas clearly
- Join in discussions
- Research and make notes
- Present information clearly

A Match the pictures on pages 44 and 45 to the correct word below.

a drought   **c** flooding   **e** lightning

b tornado   **d** sandstorm

Flooding

A flood is when a large amount of water covers what is normally dry land. Flooding usually happens when there has been heavy rainfall and natural waterways can't carry the extra water, so water overflows onto the land. In coastal areas, flooding is often caused by storms like tropical storms or tsunamis happening at the same time as high tides.

B 1 Work in groups of four. Look at the definition of flooding. Choose one each of the remaining four weather conditions from activity A. Research the condition to find out what it is and why it happens.

    2 Take turns to explain your weather condition to your group. Listen carefully to each others' explanations and ask questions if you don't fully understand. Give feedback, saying which information was clear, which was confusing and which was not useful or needed.

C Decide which of your four explanations was the clearest. Write an accurate definition in as few words as possible.

The Tempest

The Tempest is a play by William Shakespeare about betrayal, love and forgiveness. It is set on an imaginary island in the Mediterranean where Prospero, the former Duke of Milan, and his beautiful daughter, Miranda, live with their servant, Ariel.

Main characters

Prospero, former Duke of Milan	Miranda, daughter of Prospero	Ariel, a servant working for Prospero

Alonso, King of Naples	Ferdinand, son of Alonso	Antonio, Duke of Milan and brother of Prospero

Synopsis

1 A ship is being flung around by colossal waves in a violent storm. There are flashes of thunder and lightning overhead. On board the ship are Alonso, King of Naples and his son Ferdinand. Also on board is Alonso's friend Antonio, Duke of Milan and other courtiers. As the storm worsens, the crew tell the noblemen to go below out of danger. The crew struggle as the boat is tossed this way and that, then cries of panic are heard as the boat begins to sink.

On a nearby deserted island, Prospero and his beautiful daughter, Miranda, stand watching the ship sinking in the storm. She worries for those on board. Prospero tells her a story about their past and what happened 12 years ago.

Glossary

synopsis brief summary of the main events of a play, book or film

Think of a book you have read recently. Give a synopsis of the book to your partner. Say whether you would recommend the book or not, and explain why or why not.

The Tempest Act I, Scene I

(Lights flash on, then off with a clap of loud thunder, then light up part of the deck of a ship at sea in the middle of a storm. The Captain stands holding tight to the helm as he rocks back and forth with the boat. First mate and Second mate walk unsteadily to the Captain.)

FIRST MATE   The storm is growing stronger by the minute!

SECOND MATE   Ay, ay, that's for sure. I doubt we'll stay up much longer!

FIRST MATE   What! Captain! Captain! Is the ship close to land?

CAPTAIN   Uh-huh. Too close I fear…to the rocks, not the sand!

(Lights flash off, then back on with another clap of loud thunder.)

SECOND MATE   I'm not afraid of a little storm! I laugh in your face, Neptune! Ha-ha-ha…

(An enormous wave knocks Second mate from the deck into the ocean.)

SECOND MATE   Ahhhhhhhh!*(Second mate exits.)*

FIRST MATE   Tell me straight now, Captain, is the ship going down? Because I never learned to swim!

(Enter Alonso, Antonio, Ferdinand and some courtiers, all very wobbly as the waves crash onto deck.)

ALONSO   See here! As your king, I demand you to make this boat steady!

CAPTAIN   And dear **sire**, as your Captain, I ask you to leave the sailing to me!

ANTONIO   How dare you talk to the king like that!

CAPTAIN   If I don't concentrate, the king will be sleeping with the fishes!

FIRST MATE   So go back to your **cabins** now.

ANTONIO   Let's leave these **good-for-nothing** rampallions to **commandeer** the **vessel**. The storm is getting stronger now.

Glossary

sire word formerly used when speaking to a king

cabins small rooms on a ship for sleeping

good-for-nothing lazy

commandeer take control

vessel ship or boat

- Compare a synopsis text with a playscript
- Identify the features of playscripts

(The party exits except for Ferdinand.)

FERDINAND	Is there anything I can do to help on deck?
CAPTAIN	It's too dangerous. Get yourself below, young sir! The storm is worsening!

(Ferdinand reluctantly exits.)

FIRST MATE	We're turning about!
CAPTAIN	Right into a **tidal wave**! Oh, look out!

*(Captain and First mate **cower** in fear as lights down to the sound of a massive wave crashing into the ship and the shouts and cries of the crew and passengers being **enveloped** by the storm, which slowly fades just to the sound of strong wind. The stage remains dark except for a spotlight on the faces of Miranda and Prospero far right staring towards centre stage.)*

MIRANDA	Father, we must do something quickly before they all **perish** in the sea. Poor **desperate** souls!
PROSPERO	Hmm! Let me tell you a little story about **betrayal**, my dear.

Glossary

tidal wave huge sea wave moving with the tide
cower crouch down when you are afraid
enveloped covered completely
perish die
desperate hopeless
betrayal breaking the trust of another

A **Read and respond**

1 In what ways are the synopsis text and the playscript text the same? How are they different?

2 Identify the following playscript features in the extract on page 47 and above:

- Directions are written in present tense
- The speaker's name is written in the left-hand margin
- Settings are described in note form
- A description is given of how the characters speak and behave
- All directions are written in italics
- Characters' names in the directions are written in capital letters
- All directions are in brackets.

?

Imagine that you are putting on a modern version of a play that was written over 400 years ago. What changes will you need to make? Think of people's attitudes. Have some ideas changed so much that it is impossible to portray them in the present?

- Discuss how plays portray settings and characters
- Investigate where words come from

3 Find examples of interjections. Why are they used? Can you think of other commonly used interjections?

4 What do we learn about each of the characters from this short extract?

5 Explain what the following words or phrases mean:
- a clap of
- back and forth
- tell me straight
- sleeping with the fishes
- cower in fear
- rampallion

6 How is the setting of a ship at sea created? How is tension slowly built up in the scene?

B Read and perform

Practise reading the dialogue in groups of four. One person can take on the roles of Antonio, Alonso and Ferdinand (with different voices!) The other students can be First mate, Second mate and the Captain. Perform your scene in front of another group. Listen to their performance. Give each other feedback.

C What do you think?

Many English words originated from other languages. Where do you think the words **monsoon**, **tornado**, **tempest** and **iceberg** originally came from? Use an etymological dictionary to help you find out. You can find one on the internet.

Stretch zone

Find out where the words below originally came from. Use the etymological dictionary to help you.
guitar, sofa, luck, umbrella, orchestra

49

• Read a synopsis of a Shakespeare play

Synopsis *(continued)*

The Tempest

2 Twelve years ago, Prospero was the Duke of Milan and Miranda was a princess. However, they were <u>betrayed</u> by his brother, Antonio, and the King of Naples, who sent Prospero and his small daughter far out to sea on a rotten, old boat. Amazingly, they survived and washed up on the island. Since then, Prospero has waited for the opportunity of **revenge.** One day, Prospero rescues Ariel. In <u>gratitude</u>, Ariel joins with Prospero. It is Ariel who conjures up the tempest which causes the shipwreck and brings Prospero's enemies to the island.

3 After telling his story, Prospero talks to Ariel. Ariel explains that he has landed the passengers safely on different parts of the island. He has left the King's son, Ferdinand, by himself. Prospero asks Ariel to bring Ferdinand to him. Ariel <u>lures</u> Ferdinand to him with music while Prospero hides. Miranda has been sleeping, but when she hears the music she wakes up, sees Ferdinand, and the two fall instantly in love.

4 Meanwhile, hungry and <u>bedraggled</u>, Alonso, Antonio and some noblemen are stranded on another part of the island. Alonso is heartbroken because he believes his son is dead. As Alonso and his party search for Ferdinand, they are chased by wild animals, and then suddenly Ariel appears as a huge bird. He tells Alonso and Antonio they are being punished for their sins. They are terrified and run away, screaming.

5 On the other side of the island, a delighted Prospero agrees that Ferdinand can marry his daughter. He asks Ariel to bring everyone together and prepare a special **masquerade banquet**. Ariel tells Prospero that Alonso and Antonio were deeply upset by what the huge bird said and are suffering terribly. Prospero sends Ariel to bring them and the other noblemen to him. Alone, Prospero questions the right course of action: punishment or forgiveness? Is it time to move on and return home…?

Glossary

revenge hurting or harming someone in return for an injury or wrong they did to you

masquerade banquet a celebration feast where the guests wear masks

3F Playscripts Reading and comprehension

- Use the context to work out the meaning of words
- Order the events in the text
- Find evidence in the text to support ideas
- Use evidence in the text to predict what happens next

A Listen and respond

Put the following events in the order that they happen.

- Ariel scares Alonso and Antonio.
- Ariel fetches Ferdinand, who falls in love with Miranda.
- The passengers are washed up safely on different parts of the island.
- Alonso, Antonio and the courtiers are chased by wild animals.
- Alonso is miserable as he believes his son is dead.
- Prospero tells Miranda that he made Ariel create the storm.
- Ariel conjures up a huge storm to scare Alonso and Antonio.
- A ship is caught in a tempest and sinks.

B Read and respond

Support your answers with evidence from the text.

1 Use the context to work out the meaning of the underlined words.
2 Do you think Alonso and Antonio expected Prospero and his small daughter to survive?
3 Why does Prospero ask Ariel to make sure the passengers are all washed ashore in different places on the island?
4 Is it part of Prospero's plan for Miranda and Ferdinand to meet and fall in love? How do you know?
5 How are Antonio and Alonso being punished?
6 Predict what happens when Prospero comes face to face with King Alonso and Antonio. How will the play end?

C What do you think?

In pairs, discuss the following: The genre of *The Tempest* is described both as a romantic comedy and a tragicomedy. Explain where the romantic, tragic and comic elements appear in the play. Look back at **ACT I, SCENE I** and find comic elements in the scene – describe them to your partner and explain why you think they are funny.

- Learn about expressing possibility

Modal verbs

Sometimes verbs are helped by other verbs called **modal verbs**.

Modal verbs can show how likely or possible something is to happen. Here are some modal verbs:

might   should   will   must   could   may   can

Examples:

- It **might** rain today. (The sky is dark and cloudy – there's a 50% chance of rain.)

- It **should** stay sunny all day. (It's sunny now and the forecast is for good weather – there's an 85% chance it stays dry.)

- We **will** get soaking wet. (We're in the park with no shelter and it's raining heavily – there's a 100% chance we will get wet.)

We can also use **adverbs** to show how likely or possible something is to happen.

- **Never** shows something will not happen, ever.
- **Surely** shows something will probably happen.
- **Perhaps** shows there is some possibility.

Examples:

- My sister **never** misses football training.
- She **surely** won't forget her football boots.
- **Perhaps** she will get on the school team.

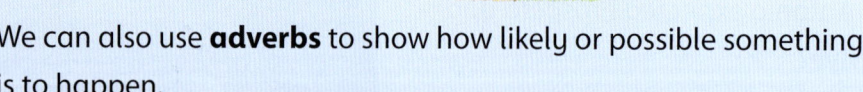

Stretch zone

In these exercises, we use modal verbs to show possibility. Write some sentences using modal verbs to show ability (he can ride a bike), permission (I can come out later), obligation (you must switch off your phones before entering).

A Write down the modal verb or adverb of possibility in each sentence.

1 The English teacher always sets lots of homework.

2 Maria should be here before the film starts.

3 Jason is running home so perhaps he is in a hurry.

4 He must be fit as he's running so fast.

5 Aisha might go to the shops with you if you ask her.

B Copy and complete these sentences with a modal verb of possibility.

1 We _____ get there in time. (We are very early.)

2 It _____ start to snow soon. (The sky is white and it's very cold.)

3 He _____ win the trophy. (He's the best player.)

4 My sister _____ be in her room. (I don't know where she is.)

5 You _____ be proud. (You came first!)

C Write five sentences showing the possibility of…

1 you going on holiday this year.

2 people living on Mars in the future.

3 meeting your friends at the weekend.

4 people using greener energy.

5 you winning a million pounds.

Commas, dashes and brackets

Writers use punctuation to separate words, phrases or clauses to make the meaning clearer for the reader.

Examples:

Commas: King Alonso was returning home from visiting his daughter, who had just got married, when the boat sank.

Dashes: Miranda sees a beautiful young man – Ferdinand – walking towards her and instantly falls in love.

Brackets: Antonio (Duke of Milan) is Prospero's younger brother.

- Commas separate a phrase or clause from the rest of the sentence. In the example above, the extra clause adds information: Alonso's daughter has just got married.

- By adding a dash instead of a comma, the added information is emphasised. In the sentence above, the reader's attention is drawn to the fact that it is Ferdinand who Miranda is in love with.

- Brackets do the opposite of dashes – they decrease the importance of the added information. Brackets give extra information without breaking the flow of the sentence.

A Write the sentences below twice. First, use dashes to separate the underlined phrase. Then use brackets.

1 Ariel <u>following Prospero's instructions</u> created a wild tempest.

2 Fifteen-year-old Miranda <u>who had never seen another man apart from her father</u> fell instantly in love with Ferdinand.

3 Prospero saved a sprite <u>Ariel</u> from imprisonment.

B Place the extra information in brackets at a suitable point in the sentence. Use brackets, commas or dashes to separate the phrase or clause you have added.

1 William Shakespeare is a famous playwright. (1564–1616)

2 The Tempest was written in 1611. (thought to be one of Shakespeare's last plays)

3 Antonio plotted with Alonso to become Duke of Milan. (Prospero's own brother)

4 Ferdinand had seen many young ladies at court but fell instantly in love with Miranda and agreed to marry her. (who was extremely pretty)

Writing workshop

Synopsis *(continued)*

6 Alonso and Antonio cannot believe that Prospero is still alive. Prospero **confronts** each of the men in turn, reminds them of their sins and then forgives them. Alonso is **repentant** and **reinstates** Prospero as Duke of Milan. Antonio says nothing. Alonso is delighted when Prospero reveals that his son, Ferdinand, is alive and engaged to Miranda. Prospero invites them all to the masquerade banquet. When the celebration is **in full swing**, Ariel disappears to repair the ship and fetch the crew together. As the celebration comes to an end, Prospero says his goodbyes to Ariel with a final request for calm seas and light winds. Then they all leave on the ship for Milan.

Glossary

confronts challenges someone face-to-face
repentant sorry
reinstates puts back into a job or position
in full swing in progress

A Read and respond

1 What do you think about the ending? Was Prospero right to forgive Alonso and Antonio rather than take revenge on them?

2 Why do you think Prospero secretly planned for Miranda and Ferdinand to marry?

3 How do you think Antonio feels about his brother being alive? Why do you think that?

B Writing a playscript

1 In pairs, write your own Shakespeare playscript. Choose one of the scenes described in the synopsis texts (2-6) and turn it into a playscript. Use the example on page 47 to help you use the correct layout. Write your first version in rough. Exchange your scene with another pair. Have they used all the correct features of playscripts? Is the dialogue realistic? Have they included any humorous scenarios? Give each other feedback.

2 Using the feedback, write out the final version of your scene.

C Performance

1 Organise a performance of your playscript for the rest of the class.

2 Watch other synopses and clips from performances of *The Tempest* being performed online.

Revise and check (1)

Vocabulary

1 **Use the context to explain the meaning of the underlined words.**

  a The brown leaves blew off the tree and <u>fluttered</u> to the ground.

  b The three <u>siblings</u> walked from home to school together each day.

  c The famous actor walked through town in <u>disguise</u> and no one recognised her.

2 **Write a sentence that includes each of the following phrases.**

  a foolish behaviour

  b masquerade party

  c worthy cause

3 **Write a definition of each of the underlined words.**

  a a <u>raging</u> storm

  b a dangerous <u>stunt</u>

  c care <u>passionately</u>

  d <u>billowing</u> flag

Punctuation

1 **Add a colon, semicolons and a full stop to this sentence.**

This is the shopping list two fresh tomatoes one packet of dried noodles 500 grams of strong cheese one kilo of small oranges a small bag of white rice

2 **Add the correct punctuation to these sentences.**

  a The famous cycling competition known as the Tour de France goes through some magnificent scenery.

  b The cyclists wind their way through several mountain ranges including The Alps and The Pyrenees during the different stages of the race.

Grammar

1 Choose the correct subordinating conjunction to complete these sentences.

> which   what   since   where   that   why   who   when

   a The house _____ my friend lives has a blue door, _____ will be painted red tomorrow.

   b I haven't seen her _____ last week _____ she fell off the wall after school.

2 Make up three sentences using the clause 'when I am hungry' in a different place in each sentence.

3 Do each of these sentences have a single clause, a main and subordinate clause, or two main clauses?

   a She ate her dinner, her father's specialty of curry, before doing her homework.

   b Maria says the delivery man has been, so we can have cream with our coffee.

   c He walked to school with his heavy bag over his shoulder.

4 Choose two modal verbs from the list below to add to this sentence.

> should   will   can   must

You _____ do your homework, so that you _____ watch your favourite programme later.

5 Add the correct prefix to these words to make another word with the opposite meaning: in- or un-.

> efficient   acceptable   believable   correct
> explained   fasten   sensitive   do   disposable

Spelling

1 Complete these words with the correct spelling of the /shun/ sound.

> -cian   -ssion   -tion

musi_____   discu_____   direc_____

opti_____   expre_____   attrac_____

4 Traditional tales and fables

"Don't put all your eggs in one basket."
Traditional moral

Talk time

1 The pictures on these pages are from traditional stories from around the world. Are any familiar to you? Do you know the stories?

2 What are the most popular stories in your country?

3 Choose one of the pictures and tell a partner what you think the story might be about.

4A Fiction Comprehension

- Discuss traditional folk tales and fables
- Tell a story
- Think of a moral for your story

A Match the story extracts (1–6) to the illustrations (A–F) on pages 58 and 59.

1 "Wolf! Wolf! The Wolf is chasing the sheep!" cried the boy.

2 Mr Dongguo took pity on the creature and offered to hide him in one of the bags strapped to his donkey.

3 Two powers, Elephant and Rain, had a **dispute**. Elephant said, "If you say that you **nourish** me, how do you do so?"

4 Unable to free himself, he filled the forest with his angry roaring. The mouse quickly found the lion struggling in the net.

5 As the girl makes her way through the forest, the wolf approaches her and asks where she is going.

6 The raven felt **flattered** by the fox's compliments and opened his beak very wide to let out a **shrill** sound. At the same time, the cheese fell out and landed in front of the fox.

B These are the opening and closing lines of the story about the mouse and lion.

Beginning: One day, a lion caught a mouse between its claws. "Please," said the mouse, "let me go and I'll come back and help you some day." The lion laughed and laughed. "You are so tiny. How could you possibly help me, the mighty lion?"

Ending: The lion turned to the mouse and said, "My dear friend. I was so wrong to **ridicule** you for being small. You truly did help me."

With a partner, talk through the events that take place between the beginning and end of the story. Your ideas should clearly show why the two animals become friends by the end and why the lion changes his opinion about the mouse.

C 1 Can you think of a moral for your story?

> A moral is a message or a lesson learnt from a story.

2 Share your story with another pair. Do they agree with the moral you have chosen for your story?

Glossary

dispute argument or disagreement

nourish keep something alive by feeding it

flattered felt good because someone said nice things

shrill high-pitched sound

ridicule tease

E

F

Read this traditional folk tale.

The Tiger and the Frog

Long, long ago, there lived an old tiger called Tsuden. He was too old to hunt large animals, so instead he tried his luck with small creatures living by the river. As he crept silently along the riverbank, a frog saw him.

5 The frog was terrified! He thought: "That's Tsuden! He's going to gobble me up. I must think of something quickly!" The frog climbed up on a large mound of mud. When Tsuden came near, the frog called out cheerfully, "Good day to you, Tsuden. How are you?"

10 Tsuden answered wearily, "I'm so hungry. I haven't eaten for days and I'm weak. You're small, but you'll make a nice snack. I'll be polite and ask who you are before I eat you, though."

Frog swelled himself up as big as he could and said very grandly, "I am the king of the frogs. I can do anything! I can jump
15 further than anyone. Let's see who can jump across this river."

Tsuden thought, "Silly frog – he can't jump further than me." And so he agreed.

As Tsuden was getting ready to leap across the river, the frog quietly hopped behind him and grabbed hold of the tiger's tail
20 in his mouth. When Tsuden leapt across the river in one huge bound, the frog held on to his tail tightly.

Tsuden landed gracefully, then turned and looked back across the river for the frog.

"Who are you looking for?" the frog asked.

25 Tsuden spun around in amazement! "How did you do that?" he demanded.

The frog just smiled. "That was a bit easy. Let's try something harder." But just then, he coughed and spat out a ball of tiger hair.

Tsuden was astonished. "Where did that come from?"
30 he asked.

The frog grinned. "Oh, a few days ago I killed and ate a tiger."

Tsuden thought nervously to himself, "That little frog killed and ate a tiger? And he jumped all
35 the way across this wide river? He really can do anything! I'd better leave, before he gobbles me up!" Then Tsuden quickly turned and sped away as fast as he could, up the mountain.

Comprehension

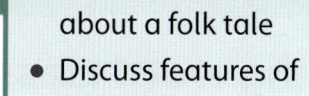

A Listen and respond

1 How does the frog feel when he sees Tsuden?

2 What test does the frog challenge the tiger to?

3 How does the frog trick the tiger?

B Read and respond

1 How does the frog make himself seem more important?
Give two ways.

2 How is the frog able to spit out tiger hairs?

3 Why do you think the frog smiles and grins when he
replies to Tsuden's questions?

4 Write a list of the common features of traditional folk tales.
Use 'The Tiger and the Frog' and other traditional folk tales
you know to help you.

C What do you think?

Read this proverb.

> The tall, strong pine is a great help, for with its support,
> the weak vine may climb as high.

1 What do you think the proverb means? How is the proverb
relevant to 'The Tiger and the Frog'?

2 Do you know any other folk tales where a character who is
weak but clever tricks a stronger character?

3 Do you know any modern stories about a weaker
character outsmarting others? Would you
recommend any of these stories to your
partner to read? Why?/Why not?

Revising word classes

Most words have more than one meaning. Look at a word in context to work out its meaning. For example, you can:

- **run** a mile (meaning: to move fast)
- **run** a business (meaning: to organize)

Every word also belongs to a **word class**. There are four main word classes: **verb**, **noun**, **adjective** and **adverb**; and four other word classes: **determiner**, **preposition**, **pronoun** and **conjunction**.

Many words belong to more than one word class. Look at a word in context to work out its word class.

Examples:

- You can **run** a mile before breakfast. (word class: verb)
- You can go on a **run** before breakfast. (word class: noun)

A Work in pairs. Match the word class with its correct use.

Word class	Use
noun	replaces a noun or shows possession of something/someone
adjective	shows an action or a state
pronoun	comes before a noun and any of its adjectives; it tells you which one, how many or how much
conjunction	used before a noun or pronoun to show place, direction or time
verb	used for people, places, ideas or things
adverb	joins words, phrases, clauses or sentences
determiner	gives more information about a verb, adjective or adverb
preposition	describes nouns

B The following words can be used in more than one word class. Write a sentence using the word in the word class given in brackets. The first one has been done for you.

break (verb) <u>I didn't mean to break your favourite cup!</u>

break (noun)_____

stop (verb) _____

stop (noun)_____

mobile (adjective)_____

mobile (noun)_____

C **1** Read this fable.

The crow and the jug

A crow, faint with thirst, found a jug which was a quarter-filled with water, but when he put his beak into the jug to try to get some water, he could not reach it. He tried and tried, but at last gave up in despair. Then he had a clever
5 thought! He dropped a pebble into the jug. Then he took another pebble and dropped it in. He took another pebble … and another … and another … and another … and so on. At last, the water rose up far enough for the crow to reach. He drank greedily and saved his life.

2 Find an example of each of the word classes below in the text.

noun		verb	
adjective		adverb	
pronoun		determiner	
conjunction		preposition	

⊙ Stretch zone

Write a sentence using one or more words from each word class. *For example:* The hungry tiger greedily ate berries which he found on a bush.

Peter and the Wolf (Part 1)

Early one morning, while his grandfather still lay sleeping, Peter sneaked quietly into the back garden, unlocked the huge, wooden gate and slipped into the lush, green meadow behind his grandfather's old cottage. On a branch of a big tree sat a little bird, Peter's friend. "All is quiet," <u>chirped</u> the bird happily.

5 Just then, a duck came <u>waddling</u> round from the garden. She was pleased that the gate had been left open and decided to take a nice, cool bath in the deep pond in the meadow.

Seeing the duck, the little bird flew down to the grass, settled next to her and shrugged. "What kind of bird are you if you can't fly?" he <u>mocked</u>. To this the duck

10 replied, "What kind of bird are you if you can't swim?" and dived into the pond. They <u>squabbled</u> and squabbled, the duck swimming in the pond and the little bird hopping excitedly along the shore.

Suddenly, something caught Peter's attention. He noticed a cat <u>crawling</u> through the grass.

15 The cat thought <u>slyly</u> to itself: "That little bird is busy arguing. I'll grab him while he's not looking." Slowly, the cat crept towards the bird on her <u>velvet</u> paws. "Look out!" screamed Peter.

In a <u>flurry</u>, the bird flew up into the tree, while the duck quacked angrily at the cat from the middle of the pond.

20 The cat licked its paw then walked <u>nonchalantly</u> around the tree, calculating to itself, "Is it worth climbing up so high? By the time I get there the bird will have flown away."

Just then, Peter's grandfather came out. He was in a furious <u>rage</u> because Peter had gone into the meadow, despite being told over and over again never to leave the back garden. "It's a dangerous place. If a wolf should come out of the forest, then what

25 would you do?" But Peter ignored his grandfather's angry words. Boys like him are not afraid of wolves! However, his grandfather grabbed Peter roughly by the hand, pulled him back home and locked the gate.

- Work out the meaning of words using context
- Learn how writers build up characters

Comprehension

A **Listen and respond**

1 Where does Peter go?

2 Who is already there?

3 Who follows Peter through the gate?

4 Why are the duck and bird unaware of the cat until Peter shouts?

5 Who is angry with Peter?

6 Is this story told from the point of view of one character, or an omniscient (all-seeing) narrator? How can you tell?

B **Read and respond**

With a partner, match each of the underlined words in the extract with one of the definitions below. Use a dictionary to help you.

a sudden period of activity or excitement

b teased

c moving secretly trying not to be noticed

d to walk with short steps, swaying or rocking from side to side

e made a short, sharp sound

f soft and smooth

g in a clever but dishonest way

h acting in an unconcerned, casual manner

i took part in a silly, unimportant argument

j showing a lot of emotion or agitation

C **What do you think?**

Discuss the following questions in pairs.

1 How does the writer build up our understanding of the characters?

2 *'Boys like him are not afraid of wolves.'* What does this tell us about the character of Peter? Discuss the following with your partner and decide whether you agree or disagree:

- He is proud, but also fearless.
- He is too young to understand the danger.
- He can't imagine what might go wrong.
- He is too relaxed and should be more concerned about his safety.

Stretch zone

Write your own sentences using the underlined words in the extract.

- Use vocabulary to make writing exciting
- Find synonyms

Shades of meaning

Look at the colour chart. All the colours are different shades of blue. Some are light, pale shades; some are strong, dark shades, but they are all shades of blue.

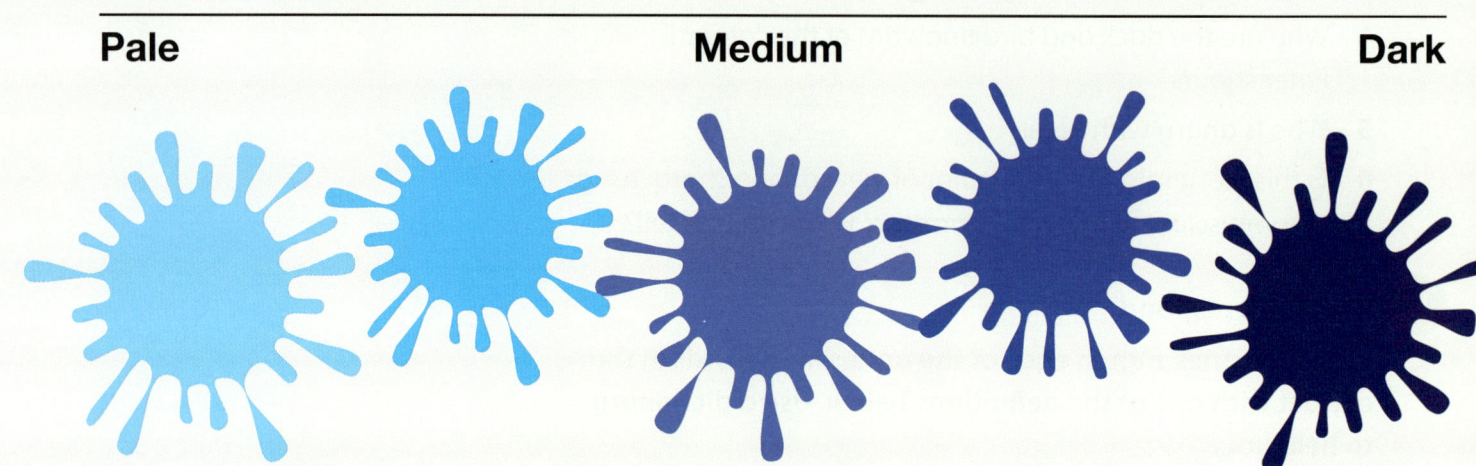

Pale   **Medium**   **Dark**

Words can act in a similar way. A number of words can have the same general meaning but some have lighter shades of meaning and some stronger.

For example: disgruntled, cross and furious all mean angry but furious has a stronger shade of meaning than cross. Someone who is furious is a lot more angry than someone who is cross. On the other hand, disgruntled has a lighter shade of meaning than cross. Someone who is disgruntled is only a little bit cross.

 1   Work in pairs. Look at the following verbs. They all mean 'to move', but at different speeds, from walking to running.

> amble   hurtle   trot   march   charge

Use a dictionary to look up the meaning of the verbs. See if you can decide where they should go on the line below, depending on the speed.

plod   sprint

Slowest ———————————————————— **Fastest**

2 Below are some adjectives that can be placed on two different shades of meaning lines. Look the words up in a dictionary, then decide where they should be placed on the lines.

tiny   upbeat   wretched   enormous   tearful
cheerful   vast   average   OK   minuscule

microscopic ↑   colossal ↑

Smallest ─────────────────────────────── **Largest**

heartbroken ↑   overjoyed ↑

Saddest ─────────────────────────────── **Happiest**

B To describe a setting well, it is important to choose adjectives carefully to make sure they convey the meaning you want.

Read the description of an untidy, deserted house. As you read, you will be given a choice of adjectives to describe the setting. Choose the adjective that you think is the most appropriate.

No one had lived in the farmhouse for years. There was a pile of (unclean/filthy) clothes on the floor in the corner of the kitchen. A pair of (muddy/grubby) boots still stood next to the back door. The kitchen was the (untidiest/muddiest) room I'd ever seen. How had the farmer managed to find things? Magazines were piled in heaps on the table, with packets of cereal and a box of hand tools. Books lay on (dusty/grotty) shelves and the floor was a (mucky/dirty) brown colour. A little light came through the (grimy/dirty) windows, which were covered on the outside with climbing plants.

C Use adjectives to describe a neglected, untidy place. It could be an old house or apartment building, or a garden. Use words and phrases from activity B. If you need to, use the picture on this page to give you some ideas.

Peter and the Wolf (Part 2)

No sooner had Peter gone, than a big grey wolf DID come out of the forest. Suddenly, everything changed.

In a twinkling, the cat **darted** up the tree. The **frantic** duck quacked and quacked and, in her panic, jumped out of the
5 pond. She ran and ran and ran as fast as she could. But no matter how hard she tried to run, she couldn't escape the wolf. He was catching up with her, getting nearer and nearer until … he caught her!

And with one gulp, he swallowed her.

10 So now, this is how things stood: the cat was sitting on one branch, the bird on another – not too close to the cat! And the large, hungry wolf walked **menacingly** around and around the tree.

Peter, without any fear, had been standing behind the closed
15 gate watching all that was going on. Then he ran home, got a strong rope, and climbed up a high stone wall.

One of the branches of the tree stretched out over the wall. Grabbing hold of the branch, Peter carefully lowered himself on to the tree. He then edged along the branch until he
20 reached the bird. Peter whispered to the bird: "Fly down and circle over the wolf's head. Only take care that he doesn't catch you."

The little bird flew down so close that he almost touched the wolf's head with his wings. The wolf snapped and **lashed
25 out** furiously at the bird, from this side and that. *Snap, snap, snap.* If only he could get hold of the bird … but the little bird was simply too quick.

Meanwhile, unbothered by the **commotion** below, Peter made a **lasso** and steadily lowered it down. The wolf was
30 not aware of the rope because he was still striking out this way and that at the bird. Peter slowly positioned the lasso and waited for the right moment. Suddenly, Peter lassoed the wolf's tail and pulled the rope tight with all his might.

Glossary

darted ran quickly

frantic panicked

menacingly threatening to cause harm

lashed out suddenly attacked

commotion great noise or excitement

lasso rope with a loop on the end

frenzy wild anger or excitement

- Look at a writer's vocabulary choice
- Discuss how tension is built up

Feeling himself caught, the wolf began to twist violently, in
35 a **frenzy** to get loose. But Peter tied the other end of the rope
to the tree, and the wolf's jumping and twisting only made
the rope around his tail tighter.

Just then, some hunters came out of the woods. They had
been following the wolf's trail. But Peter, sitting in the tree,
40 called down: "Stop! Bird and I have already caught the wolf.
Now help us take him to the zoo."

Now, imagine the triumphant procession: Peter at the
head; after him the hunters leading the wolf; and, at the
end, Grandfather and the cat. Grandfather shook his head
45 discontentedly. "What if Peter hadn't caught the wolf?
What then?"

Above them flew Birdie chirping merrily. "My, what brave
fellows we are, Peter and I! Look what we have caught!"

Comprehension

A Listen and respond

1 Why does the duck leave the pond?

2 Where is the cat?

3 What happens to the duck?

B Read and respond

1 Why is 'DID' capitalised (line 1)? How does this link back to the first extract
and what Peter's grandfather said?

2 How does the writer build up excitement when the wolf is chasing the duck?

3 Why is a dash used in line 11?

4 How does the writer build up tension in the scene where the bird is distracting
the wolf while Peter is lowering the lasso?

C What do you think?

Discuss the following questions with your partner.

1 How does the writer's choice of words help the reader to imagine the sense
of danger and threat created by the wolf's presence?

2 Do you think Peter was right to stop the hunters killing the wolf and to take
it to the zoo instead?

3 Discuss how each of the main characters (Peter, the bird, Grandfather, the
wolf) feel as they walk in the procession to the zoo.

Description of characters

- Create character profiles
- Listen to music which represents characters
- Watch an animation

A **1** Work in pairs. Read both *Peter and the Wolf* extracts again on pages 64 and 68. Then copy and complete the table using words and phrases connected with each of the characters.

Peter	sneaked, slipped
Bird	little, chirped happily
Duck	
Cat	
Grandfather	

2 Use the information in the table to write notes and build up a character profile of each of the characters. Use the given information and add your own ideas so that you build up a detailed image of each of the characters. Consider how they look, speak and move, what their personality is like and how they react to each other.

3 Share and combine your ideas with another pair. Give each other feedback and make suggestions on how the profiles could be further improved.

4 Listen to the introduction of Serge Prokofiev's *Peter and the Wolf*, where each character is represented by a different instrument. Does the instrument and tune of each of the characters fit the character profiles you created?

5 Watch clips from different films and animated versions of *Peter and the Wolf*. How are the characters portrayed? Which version do you like the most? Why?

Adjectives and adverbs

Adjectives provide more information about a noun. Commas are often used to separate the adjectives, except for the one next to the noun.

Example: Peter unlocked the **huge**, **wooden** gate and slipped into the **lush**, **green** meadow.

A **1** Find six more adjectives (and their nouns) in the extracts from *Peter and the Wolf*.

2 Add two adjectives before each of the following nouns.

a a _____ man

b a _____ dog

c a _____ door

d a _____ house

An **adverb** provides more information about a verb. It tells us how, when, where, why or under what conditions something happens or happened.

Example: Peter sneaked **quietly** into the back garden.

Sometimes more than one word does the job of an adverb. This is called an **adverbial**.

Example: **With one gulp**, he swallowed her.

B **1** Find six more adverbs (and their verbs) in the extracts from *Peter and the Wolf*.

2 Add an adverb before or after the following verbs.

a He spoke _____ on the topic of homework.

b She crept _____ down the stairs.

c _____, he went back home.

d The cat crept _____ up to the little bird.

C Correct the following sentences, replacing the adverbs with adjectives.

1 Mohamed seemed sadly.

2 The milk went badly.

3 The sea turned roughly.

4 The cake tastes well.

The /k/ sound

Spelling the /k/ sound

Some sounds are the same, but are formed by different letters. For example, the letters **ck**, **k**, **ke**, **c** and **que** at the end of words all make a /k/ sound.

- When the /k/ sound comes straight after a short vowel sound, we usually spell it **ck** as in sa**ck**, pe**ck**, thi**ck**et and so**ck**et.

- When the /k/ sound comes after another consonant, we usually use **k** as in bas**k**et, sil**k**, blan**k** or par**k**.

- When the /k/ sound is in the middle of a split digraph (e.g. **a-e**, **o-e**, **i-e**), we usually use **k** as in ra**k**e, sna**k**e, po**k**e or spi**k**e.

- Some words originally came from the French language and end with a /k/ sound made by **que**. Examples of this include anti**que** or uni**que**.

A Look at lines 1–5 of *Peter and the Wolf* (Part 2) again. How many different letter formations of the /k/ sound can you find?

B 1 Write five more examples of words with the spelling **ck**.

   2 Write five more examples of words with the spelling **k**.

   3 Write five more examples of words with the spelling **k** in the middle of a split digraph.

   4 Write one more example of a word with the spelling **que**.

C Add the correct /k/ spelling to the following words.

bar__   atta__   artwor__   kno__   earthqua__

chal__   pinpri__   mista__   hammo__   sti__

uni__   picni__   comi__   bri__   li__

Stretch zone

Try to find three other words using **que** to make the /k/ sound like antique.

Description of a setting

Describing a forest

The entrance to the forest path was like a sort of arch. It led into a gloomy tunnel made by two great trees that leant together, too old and strangled with ivy to **bear** more than a few blackened leaves. The path itself was narrow and wound in and out among the trunks. Soon the light at the gate
5 was like a little bright hole far behind. The quiet was so deep that their feet seemed to thump along while all the trees leaned over them and listened. As their eyes became used to the dimness, they could see a little way to either side in a sort of darkened green glimmer. Occasionally a **slender** beam of sun that had the luck to slip in through the leaves above, and still more luck
10 in not being caught in the tangled **boughs** and **matted** twigs beneath, stabbed down thin and bright before them. But this didn't happen often, and it soon stopped altogether. There was no movement of air down under the forest-roof, and it was still and dark and stuffy.

A 1 Find six adjectives describing what it was like to be in the forest.

2 The forest is full of trees that are very close to each other. How does the writer show this?

3 Explain why the word 'stabbed' is used to describe the sunlight.

Glossary

bear produce
slender thin
boughs branches
matted tangled

B Imagine you are deep in a thick forest when the sun is setting. What things in the forest might you see, hear, smell or touch? Add figurative language to your paragraph to make it more descriptive.

For example:

simile – The branches stretched out like twisted, gnarled fingers.

metaphor – The trees were statues standing utterly still.

onomatopoeia – crunch, crackle

alliteration – The moist, mossy mattress of the forest floor.

Can you think of a way of using personification?

C Write a paragraph describing a forest. Use powerful, descriptive words to help the reader imagine what you can see, hear, smell and touch.

Writing a modern folk tale

Write a new story about Peter and the Wolf

Peter decides not to take the wolf to the zoo but to release it back into the woods. Now Peter has another adventure. This time, the action takes place in the woods and Peter gets into serious trouble...

Work with a partner and write notes about Peter's new adventure. First, decide whose point of view your story will be told from. For example, will Peter tell the story? Will there be a narrator? Or will another character describe what happens? Plan to write at least five paragraphs using the narrative structure below to guide you. Use your character profile notes (page 70) and description of the forest (page 73) to help you with the detail.

Setting	Grab the reader's attention by writing an exciting and detailed description of the wood.
	Use powerful adjectives and verbs as well as some figurative language.
	Don't forget to describe what you can see, hear, smell and feel.
Characters	Peter, the wolf.
	The bird? The cat? Peter's grandfather?
	The hunters? A new character?
Introduction and build-up of a problem	What trouble will Peter get into?
	What danger does he face?
	Does it involve another person, an animal or maybe part of the forest, like a hidden pit or cave?
	Is the wolf involved?
Climax	What is the danger?
	What causes the danger he is in? Is it the wolf?
	Use similes and metaphors to describe the danger and short sentences to build up the tension.
Resolution	How does Peter escape/get free?
	Is the wolf the cause of the problem or does the wolf rescue Peter and save him from danger?
	Does it end happily for everyone?

Stretch zone

Try retelling your story from the point of view of another main character, such as the wolf, or a minor character, such as the bird or Grandfather.

Fiction writing workshop

1 When you are happy with your story plan, find a new partner. Take turns to talk through your stories and give each other feedback. Are the characters and setting well-described? Do events follow a logical progression from start to finish? Does the action build up to an exciting climax? Is there a satisfactory resolution? Was the story interesting to listen to all the way through? Tell your partner what you think works well and what they can do to make their narrative even better.

2 Using your partner's feedback, all of your notes and the success criteria below, write the final version of your story.

Modern folk tale success criteria

The chosen point of view is consistent throughout.
The setting is well-described (using powerful adjectives and adverbs to add interest and effect).
The characters are well-described (using powerful adjectives and adverbs to add interest and effect).
Powerful verbs are used to create exciting action.
Figurative language is used to vividly describe what can be seen, heard, smelled or felt.
Punctuation is used for effect, like an ellipsis for a dramatic pause.
A mixture of short and long sentences are used to build up tension.
The action builds up to an exciting climax.
The past tense is used consistently throughout the story.
The correct spelling, punctuation and grammar is used.
There is a satisfactory resolution, such as: Peter escapes the danger.

Narrative performance

3 Practise reading your narrative out loud. Remember to vary your expression and speed to make your reading interesting. Use different voices and actions to bring your characters alive too.

4 Read your narrative to the class. When you have given your own performance, watch the performances of your classmates. What went well and what could your classmates have done to make their reading performance even better?

5 School days

"Aim for success, not perfection. Never give up your right to be wrong, because then you will lose the ability to learn new things and move forward with your life."

David M. Burns

Talk time

1 *The Tree of Knowledge* is an old metaphor. Why do you think knowledge is shown as a tree?

2 Look at the pictures. Which clues show you that the children are on their way to, or at, school?

3 Think of a caption (a word, phrase or sentence) to describe the two pictures in circles.

Eager to learn

- Discuss why learning is important
- Discuss which subjects are important
- Try to persuade your classmates

A Which subjects do you believe are the most important to learn at school to achieve a good education? With a partner, decide which are the most important for you.

- your own language
- a foreign language
- literature
- mathematics
- science
- music
- drama
- arts and crafts
- cooking
- individual sports
- team sports
- humanities (history/geography/religious education)
- gardening
- computing

Share your ideas with the class.

B **1** Imagine you are in a hot air balloon which is losing height rapidly and will soon crash because it is too heavy. To keep the balloon in the sky, you have to remove half the passengers. You are all teachers from the same school and all teach different subjects.

2 In groups, decide which subject each of you teach. Then consider why your subject is more important than all the others. Your aim is to persuade the other teachers in the balloon that your subject is one of the most important in the school and therefore you should not be removed from the balloon.

3 Make a list of all the key points you want to use in your favour. Think of the arguments your fellow teachers might make about the importance of their own subjects and think of counter-arguments you can make against them.

C **Hold your debate. Remember to be polite and respectful to others when giving opposing views.**

Who was able to persuade the other teachers that their subject was one of the most important? How did they manage to persuade everybody? Were you convinced by your own ideas about how important a subject is? Or were you more convinced by another teacher in the balloon?

*'Yash used to be so **unmotivated**. At Jonsbourne School, he has achieved Grade 8 in piano, plays tennis for the county and gets straight As. He is **flourishing**!'*

Welcome to our school family!

- Fed up of your child getting lost in the crowd?

- Looking for a school where your child will reach their **full potential**?

- Look no further! Here at Jonsbourne School, we provide our children with a perfectly balanced education for the 21st century.
  - ✔ high academic standards
  - ✔ outstanding personal development
  - ✔ wide range of extracurricular activities
  - ✔ **exceptional** site and facilities

Through our amazing programmes of study, and our focus on each child's personal development, we create a 'can do' attitude. We teach our pupils all the key life skills they need to succeed:

- ✔ problem solving
- ✔ risk-taking
- ✔ positive mental attitude
- ✔ **resourcefulness**

We provide a warm and friendly environment. Each child feels valued and important. We will identify each child's special talents, whether that be academic, musical, theatrical, artistic, sporting – or something else – and we will help them to flourish.

We'll stretch them, we'll assist them, we'll push them to succeed!

At Jonsbourne School, we really do provide an all-round education!

Please call to make an appointment and experience the wonderful atmosphere of Jonsbourne School in person.

We look forward to meeting you.

Mrs L C Winterbottom
Headteacher

* Learn about persuasive language
* Write an advertisement

A Listen and respond

1 What is the purpose of the advertisement?

2 Who is the advertisement written by? How do you know?

3 Who is the advertisement aimed at? How do you know?

B Read and respond

1 What effect is the writer trying to achieve by using the words 'school family' in the heading?

2 Why is a quotation included in the advertisement?

3 Why does the writer use pronouns? The writer uses another technique for the same reason. What else does the writer do?

4 Why are dashes used in the text?

5 Explain what a 'can do' attitude is.

C What about you?

Discuss these questions with your partner.

1 Would you like to go to Jonsbourne School? Why/Why not?

2 Is Jonsbourne School anything like your school? Why/Why not?

3 If you were asked to write an advertisement for your school, what information would you include?

Stretch zone

Design a poster advertising all the good things about your school.

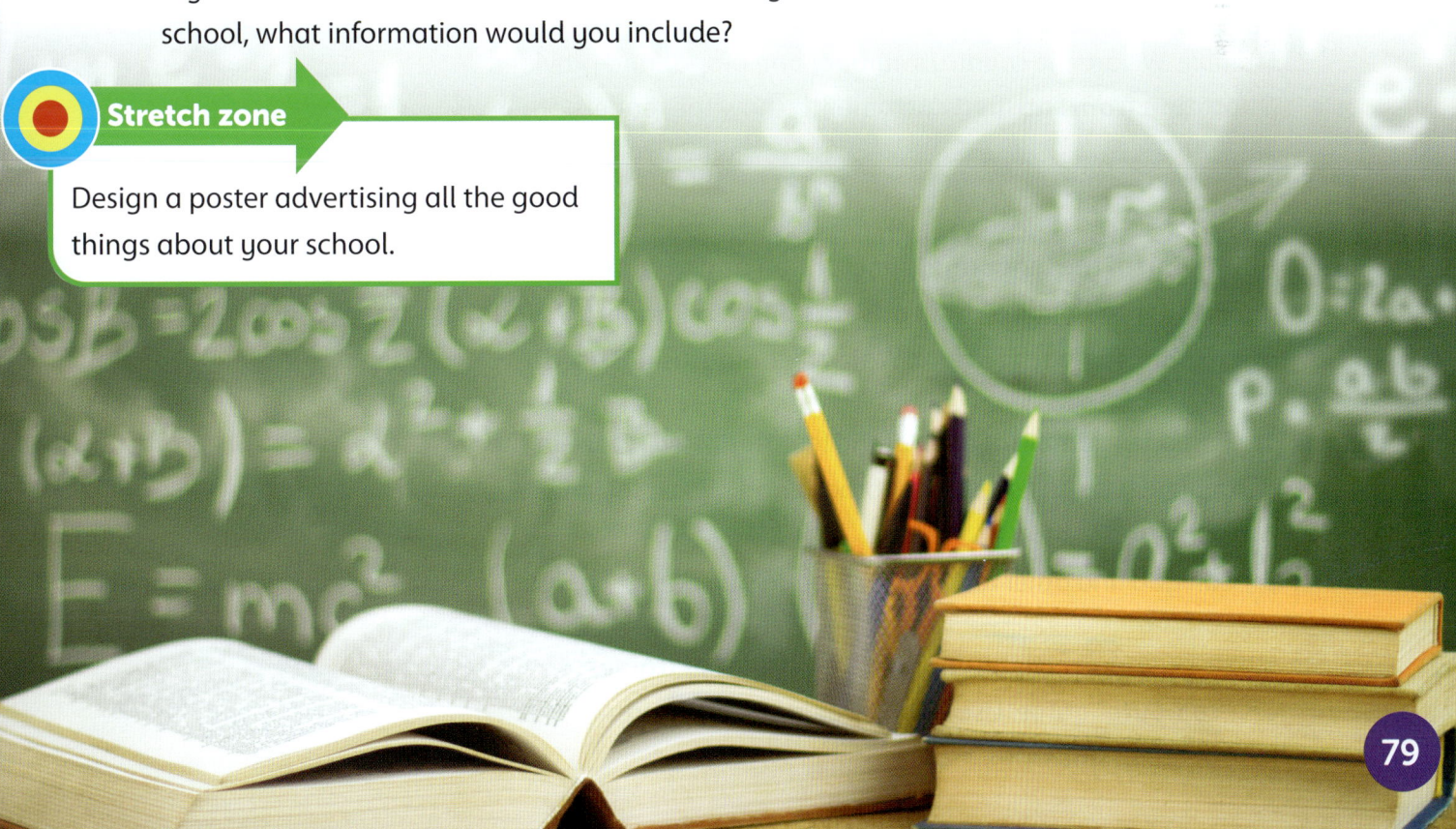

- Explore how language, grammar and punctuation influence the reader

Persuasive language

Read the language, punctuation and grammar techniques that are used for persuasive purposes.

- Use of **pronouns**, so the reader thinks the advert is directly addressed to them. *Example:* We will do all the hard work for you!
- **Short sentences** for impact. *Example:* It's so easy.
- Use of '**and**' and '**but**' to make points seem straightforward and honest. *Example:* And, what's more…
- **Contractions** creating a conversational tone. *Example:* You couldn't ask for better.
- **Adverbs** for emphasis. *Examples:* simply, naturally, just. Or to prove that something is correct. *Examples:* definitely, of course
- **Adjectives** to describe the selling point of the product. *Example:* brilliant, best, cheapest
- **Rhetorical questions**. *Example:* Unhappy with your broadband provider?
- **Alliteration** so that attention is drawn to words. *Example:* better broadband
- **Modal verbs** such as 'will', 'can' and 'could', emphasising what will be achieved. *Example:* We will change the way you view your broadband!
- **Bullet points, bold, italics** to make the information stand out. *Example:* We are the country's ***number one*** broadband provider!
- **Quotation from satisfied customer** to show the readers others are impressed with the product. *Example:* 'Really great product!'

Want to cut your broadband bills, but can't find the time because you're too busy?

- Well, just leave it to us and we will find the best deal for you. It's as easy as that!
- Simply call us free on 01800 212 212

What difference can we make?

- Top experts brought in to search the best deals for your area
- Fantastic reduction in costs

P.S. And if you don't have time today, just do it tomorrow. We will still be here. Of course we will. Because we care…

A How many of the language, punctuation and grammar features above are used in the school advertisement on page 78? Find one example of each feature. Which technique is *not* used?

B 1 Find one example of each of the features listed above in the Uconnect advertisement for broadband. Which technique is *not* used?

2 Can you find other techniques used to persuade?

C Make up an advertisement for a new brand of trainers or a computer game. Use a range of language and layout techniques.

Persuasive punctuation

Persuasive texts, such as advertisements, use a wide range of punctuation – often to make the text seem like a speaking voice.

Examples: You know it makes sense!

Want to try a different kind of computer game?

A Match the examples below with the correct punctuation mark.

Worried about your spots?	exclamation mark
We think (and we know we're right) that you will notice a difference.	semicolon
No more blocked drains!	question mark
No more unhappy wash days; no more dirty shirts.	parenthetic commas
Our service, which is second to none, will transform your home.	brackets

B Write out this text advertising an amusement park ride, adding all the missing punctuation. Try to include an example of all of the persuasive punctuation from activity A.

Are you ready for the ride of a lifetime Then climb on board You'll experience sensations you have never experienced before and I mean never You'll climb higher than you have ever been before or ever imagined possible Once at the very top of the world you'll hover just for a second just time to anticipate what is going to come next Then vroom you'll be plunging straight down breaking the speed barrier faster than the speed of light so fast it will literally take your breath away. Are you ready for the ride of a lifetime Then what are you waiting for Come on board

C Look at the advertisement you created for activity C on page 80. Change some of the punctuation so that you get the effect of a speaking voice.

Persuasive writing

To: Mrs Winterbottom

Subject: Homework

From: Mina Efron

Dear Mrs Winterbottom,

5 As a mum of three primary-aged children attending Jonsbourne School, I would like
to respond to your comment in this week's school newsletter. You complained about the fact that
some students are not completing homework tasks set by their class teachers. I understand that
you have our children's **best interests at heart**; however, I disagree with the school policy on
this subject.

10 Firstly, for young children I can find no scientific evidence that homework improves
their school grades. In fact, there are studies which show that giving homework to primary-aged
children has a negative impact. Children come home after a long and tiring day at school and
are then expected to spend further time studying. Do you know how difficult it is to get a tired child
to complete an hour-long maths assignment after they have been at school all day?

15 Moreover, I feel that homework creates too much stress in our family life. As you can
imagine, with three young children, I have a busy schedule as they all have different interests. They attend
many of the after-school clubs such as music lessons, sports training, drama classes, and more.
These are all activities, as I am sure you will agree, that are important in forming **fully-rounded** adults.
Well, homework seriously reduces the time my children have for these activities.

20 Finally, I believe it is important that children enjoy being children, by
playing with friends, having free reading time, learning life skills such as
cooking. I believe these things are more important than homework activities.

For all of the reasons above, I would like to ask for my children to be
excluded from any future homework activities. Thank you for reading
25 my email and I hope that you will understand my position. I would be
happy to discuss this matter further with you if you have any concerns.

Yours sincerely,

Mina Efron

Glossary

best interests at heart show concern and want to help someone

fully-rounded someone who is skilled, capable or knowledgeable in a lot of different things

excluded not included

Comprehension

- Discuss persuasive writing
- Identify viewpoint and purpose
- Learn how biased arguments are created

A Listen and respond

1 What do we know about the person who wrote this email?

2 Why has this email been written? Where can you find a summary of its purpose?

3 What tense is the email written in?

4 What is the purpose of the final paragraph?

B Read and respond

1 Find three examples of both of the following in the email:

   a conjunctions linking the paragraphs

   b conjunctions linking ideas within a paragraph

2 Find one example of each of the following in the email:

   a emotive words or phrases appealing to the reader

   b use of a question to the reader

3 Paragraphs 2, 3 and 4 each make a different point in the writer's argument. What is the main point of each paragraph?

C What about you?

1 Do you think homework should be banned or do you think it is a necessary part of your education?

2 The email is a biased argument. The writer only gives one side of the argument: reasons against homework. For each point that you identified in activity B, think of a counter-argument in favour of homework. Can you think of any more reasons why children should be given homework?

Biased arguments – using language to persuade

- Hold a group debate
- Present one side of an argument
- Persuade the audience

1 In this activity, you are going to have a group debate. The aim is to get the audience members in the group to agree with you. You will work in a group of six – three pairs. There will be two speakers arguing in agreement with the statement (for), two arguing against the statement and two outside the debate – one chair and one audience member.

2 Before you start debating, look at the statements below. Your teacher will tell you which statement you will argue for and which you will argue against. In pairs, make notes of all the ideas you can think of for and against each of the two statements you will debate. For each of your ideas **for** or **against**, think of a possible counter-argument too.

> - There should be at least one school trip every term.
> - Every schoolchild should learn how to play a musical instrument.
> - Young people should be banned from playing any screen games on school nights.

3 When you have enough ideas, start your debate. The two students agreeing with the statement should begin the debate by giving a reason in support of the statement. The two students against should give a counter-argument. The debate can then go back and forth.

The chairperson will control the debate and tell the sides when it is their turn to talk. Remember to be polite and to listen carefully to others when they are speaking.

The audience member will listen and ask questions at any point in the debate to clarify points.

4 When you have expressed all your ideas and finished debating one statement, the audience member will decide whether they agree or disagree with the statement.

5 All pairs swap roles and debate the next statement. Keep on going until you have discussed all three statements.

More conjunctions, adverbs and adverbials

A **conjunction** is a kind of linking word – a word or phrase that links clauses or sentences together. Conjunctions can be:

Co-ordinating – linking phrases which are equally important.
Example: I like pasta **but** my sister prefers rice.

Subordinating – linking words which are not as important (a subordinate clause) to the rest of the sentence (the main clause).
Example: Sadiq went for a walk **although** it was raining.

Conjunctions can be used to connect a main and subordinate clause, two separate clauses or two separate sentences.

Adverbs/adverbials – give more information about a verb, adjective, another adverb or clause.
Example: Jack desperately wanted to win the race. **However**, he fell down and had to be carried to the finishing line. **As soon as** his mum saw him, she gave him a big hug.

A Adverbials of time are used for instructions, recounts and sequencing. Copy and complete the passage using the appropriate adverbials of time. You might need to add capital letters.

> then   while   next   until   first   when   as soon as

How to cook an omelette

_____, pour a little oil in a frying pan and _____ wait for it to heat up. _____ the oil is heating up, carefully crack two eggs in a bowl. Add a little milk and a pinch of salt and pepper. _____ use a whisk to beat the eggs _____ they are frothy. _____ the oil is hot enough, ask an adult to pour the egg mixture into the pan. Spread it across the whole pan. _____ the egg is cooked on one side, use a spatula to flip over your omelette.

More conjunctions, adverbs and adverbials

- In biased and balanced arguments, linking words, such as conjunctions, adverbs and adverbials are very important because they help the reader follow the points and ideas. Some adverbs, such as **additionally, furthermore, as well as, also** are used to show similarity or add a point.

  Example: We shouldn't use fossil fuel because it's non-renewable. **Furthermore**, burning coal pollutes the atmosphere.

- Some linking words, such as **on the other hand, whereas, however,** are used to show difference or an opposite idea.

  Example: Homework is good for practising what you've already learnt. **However,** teachers should limit the amount they give.

- Some linking words, such as **after all, anyway, besides** are used to make a point stronger, while others such as **for example** and **for instance** are used for explaining a point with evidence.

  Example: I told my brother not to eat sweets because it makes him very excitable. **Besides**, they are bad for him. **For instance**, they can damage his teeth.

B Choose the correct linking words to complete the paragraph.

> firstly   therefore   also   next   additionally   lastly
> for example   however

Some people believe that there are lots of pros to doing sports in school. ——————, there are a number of cons too. ——————, sports can distract from our academic studies. ——————, taking part in sports can put pressure on children to be the best, and not to be a 'loser'. ——————, some non-sporty children can feel really stressed in sports lessons. ——————, there is the safety element to consider. If a child gets injured, it can cause a long-term problem. ——————, the time doing sports could be put to better use, —————— understanding equations or practising languages. ——————, I can easily do sports outside of school hours.

- Look at balanced arguments

The pros and cons of homework

Some teachers believe that giving homework is an important part of our education, while others believe that it should not be necessary for us to work at home. So, what are the pros and cons of homework?

At my school, many teachers believe that homework is vital if we are to learn everything we need to become skilled in a subject. Homework gives us the opportunity to practise the skills we learn in class. In addition to this, homework such as maths questions and spelling and vocabulary lists can help us to prepare for future lessons. Reading activities are meant to be especially important for younger children still learning the language. What is more, homework is necessary when we do not have enough time in the classroom to complete a topic or can sometimes be used to produce extended pieces of work like science projects. Lastly, it is also said that homework encourages **self-discipline** and **independence**, both of which are important lifeskills for us to learn.

On the other hand, some parents believe that homework should not be necessary. They think that too much homework is often given and this causes stress on family life. Additionally, many studies show that homework does not improve students' academic grades, especially at infant school. Moreover, if we are doing homework every night, we will have less time to develop our interests and improve our skills in other areas such as music and sports. Not only that, homework can be so stressful that it has a negative effect because it means that we don't enjoy studying. Finally, we need time just to relax and enjoy ourselves. Holidays should be a break from work. We need time off too!

As I have shown here, there are strong arguments for and against homework. In my opinion, homework does have an important part to play in education. However, it should only be given when necessary and time spent on homework should be limited to two hours per week.

Glossary

self-discipline control over oneself

independence being able to do things yourself, without relying on others

Stretch zone

Make a list of reasons why it is better to learn 'life skills' than to complete homework after school.

● Identify the viewpoint and purpose

A **Listen and respond**

1 Who is the writer of the argument? How do you know?

2 Who is the target audience? How do you know?

3 What is the purpose of the:
   ● first paragraph?
   ● second paragraph?
   ● third paragraph?
   ● last paragraph?

B **Read and respond**

1 Is the tone formal or informal? How do you know?

2 Two sentences are slightly different in tone to the rest of the text. Which two are different and what makes them different?

3 Which tense is used in the text? Explain why.

4 Look at the sentence length. Are they mainly long, short or a mixture of both? Explain why you think the writer did this.

5 The writer uses phrases such as 'parents/teachers believe…' to show that the point they're making is not their own opinion but someone else's. Find two other phrases that show it is not the writer's own opinion.

6 Make a list of the main points for and against homework in the argument.

7 All the conjunctions and conjunctive adverbials, apart from one, are used to add additional supporting information. Which one is used to introduce an opposite idea?

C **What do you think?**

Look at the statement below.

> There should be more time given to learning about music and playing a musical instrument.

Do you agree? With a partner make a list of all the pros and cons of learning more music at school.

Relative clauses and relative pronouns

A **relative clause** can be used to give additional information about a noun.

A relative clause is introduced by a **relative pronoun**, such as 'which'.

The relative pronoun is used to refer back to the noun which has already been mentioned in the sentence.

Example: This is the brilliant <u>book</u> **which** I told you about.

Relative pronouns can describe people, things (including animals) and places.

Relative pronouns include:

- **who**, referring to people
- **which**, referring to animals, places or things
- **when**, referring to a time or time period
- **where**, referring to a place
- **whose**, the possessive form of 'who'
- **that**, referring to people, places or things.

A   Match the beginning of the sentence with the correct ending.

She didn't know the person	whose brother went to school with me.
Leave your coats	when Lian gets here.
This is Marc	that I left on the chair?
What happened to the book	which she borrowed from Juray.
We're all going to the cinema	where you were told to.
Farah gave back the pencil	who sent her the flowers.

Relative clauses and relative pronouns

B Complete each of the sentences by adding one of the relative pronouns below. Each relative pronoun is used only once.

> who   which   when   where   whose   that

1   The park ——————— we play football is next to Sam's house.

2   Is Dr Khan the guy ——————— teaches Maths?

3   Who ate the apple ——————— I left on my desk?

4   Pavel will go for lunch ——————— he's finished the activity.

5   Can the child ——————— jumper is on the floor please pick it up?

6   This is the picture ——————— Lola painted for my birthday.

C Complete these sentences with an appropriate relative clause.

1   That's the old woman …

2   I like the film …

3   The teacher asked a question …

4   He has a pet …

5   His aunty is the famous actress …

6   We'll go on holiday …

Stretch zone

Work in pairs. Choose a famous person. Write a simple statement such as: Harry Potter is a wizard. Take it in turns to add more information by using a relative clause. *For example:*

Harry Potter is a wizard who attends Hogwarts.
Harry Potter is a wizard who attends Hogwarts which is a kind of secondary school.

Writing to persuade

Student A and Student B were given the following writing task.

> You are a member of the student council. You have been asked to write a speech to present to the school principal arguing for more time for sport at your school.
>
> Your aim is to persuade the principal to accept and agree with your point of view.

- Use persuasive techniques
- Write a speech
- Perform your speech

Language tips

Persuasive writing has:

- Short sentences
- Rhetorical questions
- Sets of three words or phrases
- Emotive words

Getting the right start

In this writing task, the first paragraph should tell the principal what their argument is about and what they hope to achieve. This makes it very clear to the principal at the beginning exactly what they can expect. Read Student A and Student B's introductory paragraphs below. Which one is the best start to an argument?

STUDENT A

Good morning, Principal. My name is Jacintha Thomson, and I am here today to try to persuade you to let us have more time in school for sporting activities. At present, we only have one hour a week. We think it should be increased to at least two hours a week. Here are the reasons for our request.

Correct formal address: 'Good morning, Principal. My name is...'

Says WHY she is speaking to the principal, summing up the argument. Does not go on to the reasons yet.

Gives a clear link to the next paragraph: 'Here are the reasons for...'

STUDENT B

Hi! We're getting fed up not having sport. Everyone wants more because sport keeps you fit and healthy and it also gives you other qualities like determination. So why can't we have more time?

Informal address: 'Hi!'

Does not sum up what the argument is or why they are speaking to the principal.

No link to the next paragraph.

The whole argument is covered in one paragraph!

Developing your argument

It is important that each paragraph covers only one point. Usually, you state what the paragraph is going to be about through a topic sentence.

Example: Firstly, more sport will mean that children will be fitter and healthier.

Then you go on to prove it. You can prove your topic sentence by giving:

- examples
- facts and statistics
- a personal anecdote (a 'story' of someone you know or have heard about)
- a final sentence that contrasts how things are now with how they could be in the future.

Find examples of these in the second paragraph written by Student A, below.

First, more time given to sport will mean that children will be fitter and healthier. One hour of sport a week is simply not enough. Government research shows that if children have a minimum of two hours a week of exercise, their fitness rates will go up by 40%. Surely you want this for the children in your school? I have a close friend who is overweight and unfit, and actually begged the Head of Physical Education for more sports time because he desperately wants to become fitter. The choice is yours, Sir. Fitter, healthier, happier children who enjoy two hours of sport a week – or unhealthy, unfit children who have barely enough time to enjoy one sporting slot over a whole week.

Summing up

A good conclusion will refer back to the beginning and sum up the argument:

I trust I have made a convincing argument for having two hours a week of sport in school, rather than one hour. The children in this school will be fitter, healthier, happier, and – most importantly – more capable of working hard and achieving top grades! Thank you for your time and attention.

Writing workshop

You are a member of the student council. You have been asked to write a speech to present to the school principal requesting more time for music lessons at your school.

1   Use the following table to help you structure your speech and write notes.

Paragraph	Content
Introduction	Who you are, why you're making the speech, summary of main ideas
First paragraph	Topic sentence, then facts, statistics, examples, etc.
Second paragraph	Topic sentence, then facts, statistics, examples, etc.
Third paragraph	Topic sentence, then facts, statistics, examples, etc.
Conclusion	Sum up argument, say how things might be in the future, thank the principal

2   When you have completed your notes, write a rough copy of your speech. Present it to your partner. Listen to your partner's speech. Give each other feedback using the success criteria below.

Persuasive argument speech success criteria

There is a clear introduction, stating your argument and what you hope to achieve.
Your argument builds up step-by-step in each paragraph.
You've included a topic sentence for each paragraph, which you then prove using: examples, a personal anecdote, facts and statistics, a comparison between the present and the future.
Some persuasive techniques are used, such as short sentences, rhetorical questions, humour, appealing directly to the principal.
There is a conclusion which refers back to the first paragraph and sums up the argument.

3   Using your partner's feedback and the success criteria, write the final version of your speech. When you are finished, reread your speech carefully and check for any punctuation, grammar or spelling mistakes.

4   Present your speech to your group.

6 Let's celebrate!

A

B

C

D

"Celebration is a kind of food we all need in our lives, and each individual brings a special recipe or offering, so that together we will make a great feast."

Corita Kent and Jan Steward

Talk time

1 Celebrations and festivals often include: special food, music, lights, singing and dancing, different clothes, fireworks and crowds. Find these in the pictures above.

2 Which of the celebrations in the pictures would you like to join?

3 Give three reasons why people have celebrations.

4 What festivals do you have in your country?

- Talk about world celebrations
- Describe your country's celebrations

The world loves to celebrate

A Match the photos (A–D) on page 94 with the sentences (1–4).

1 They celebrated the harvest with a musical performance.

2 The decoration on the parade float was spectacular.

3 The family celebrated the day with a birthday cake.

4 They celebrated New Year's Day with a firework display.

B 1 Put the following words in alphabetical order, then look up their meaning in a dictionary.

> fireworks   feast   harvest   float
> parade   carnival   anniversary

Use some of the words to answer questions 2 and 3.

2 Add the missing word. A f_ _ _ _ is a special meal with lots of different food that can last for days.

3 Unscramble the words and match them to their definition.

skorwerif   a celebration or party held at the same time each year

narcilav   loud, colourful explosions

varsinneray   a large, lively parade which moves through a town or city

4 Match the words to the correct word class.

celebrate	decorate	**noun**
celebrated	decorated	**verb**
celebration	decoration	**past participle verb**

C Prepare a talk about your favourite festival or celebration and present it to the class. Use the points below to help you.

- Name the celebration in your introduction.

- List its celebratory features, such as rest from work, chance for families to meet.

- Give details of the celebration, including the dates and places.

- Finish with sentences on why a visitor might want to observe this celebration and why it is your favourite.

Kwanzaa is an African-American celebration.

Dragon performance

During Chinese New Year celebrations, performers take on the costume of a dragon or lion and dance through the streets.

Dragon Dance

A Chinese dragon's in the street
And dancing on its Chinese feet
With fearsome head and golden **scale**
And twisting its **ferocious** tail.
5 Its **bulging** eyes are **blazing** red
While smoke is puffing from its head
And well you nervously might ask
What lies behind that fearful mask.
It twists and twirls across the road
10 While BANG the cracker strings explode.
Don't yell or run or shout or squeal
Or make a Chinese dragon's meal
For, where its heated breath is fired
They say it likes to be admired.
15 With slippered joy and
prancing shoe
Why, you can join the
dragon too.
There's fun with beating
20 **gongs** and **din**
When dragons dance
the New Year in.

Max Fatchen

Glossary

scale semi-circular plates protecting the skin of fish and reptiles
ferocious fierce, aggressive
bulging swelling, bigger than normal
blazing very hot
prancing moving around in a happy or lively way
gongs metal discs that make a sound when hit
din loud noise

Comprehension

A **Listen and respond**

1 What is the poet describing?

2 The poem makes reference to two colours of the dragon. What are they?

3 What background sounds does the poem describe?

B **Read and respond**

1 Find an example of the figurative techniques below in the poem:

- onomatopoeia

- alliteration

2 Find all the two-word phrases (adjective + noun) used to describe the dragon. *Example:* Chinese feet

3 The word 'fear' is used in the poem with two different suffixes. What are they? The two words are used in a similar way but they have different meanings. Use a dictionary to find their meanings. What other suffixes can you add to the word 'fear'?

4 What effect do the rhyming lines have on the rhythm of the poem? Why do you think the poet does this?

5 Which theme would you choose to sum up this poem?

a excitement

b happiness

c celebration

C 1 Do you like the poem? Give examples from the poem to explain your feelings about it.

2 Would you like to take part in a dragon dance? Explain why or why not.

97

Tricky spellings and unstressed vowels

Some words are tricky to spell because they don't follow usual spelling rules. These words need to be learned and practised. Some words have **unstressed vowels** in them. This means that the vowels (a, e, i, o, u) are not easy to hear. As a result, they are often missed out in spellings.

A All these words have unstressed vowels.

> bus**i**ness   off**e**ring   diff**e**rent   eas**i**ly   fam**i**ly
> Wedn**e**sday   int**e**rest   fright**e**ning   sep**a**rate
> gen**e**rous   marv**e**llous   mis**e**rable   gen**e**rally

1   Say the words aloud several times, stressing the underlined vowel.

2   Write the words with the underlined vowels enlarged or highlighted. This will help you to remember the vowel.

3   Write sentences using some of these words, spelling them correctly.

B Choose the correct spelling of the words in brackets to complete the sentences.

1   Ali was a (misceivous/mischievous/mischevous) little boy who loved to (embarrass/embarris/embarres) his older sister.

2   His (conschious/conscience/conshious) told him it wasn't (accepible/exceptable/acceptable) to take a (forth/fourth/fouth) cake.

3   It isn't (necesary/neccessary/necessary) to take the books back to the (library/libary/libury) (imediately/immeditely/immediately).

C Find these five difficult-to-spell words in this word search. Then write a sentence with each of the words.

> occasionally   neighbour   noticeable
> jewellery   independent

Difficult words and homophones

A   Choose ten words from the 'Tricky spellings' list that you find difficult to spell. Use these strategies to help you remember them.

- Write the word over and over again, highlighting the letters that are difficult to remember.
  Examples: sep**a**rate, ne**cess**ary

- Make personal associations. *Example:* ne**cess**ary – **c**ats **e**at **s**alty **s**ardines

- Create pictures in your head. *Example:* **c**url (not **k**url) – see a cat **c**urled in a c-shape

- Make it an acrostic. *Example:* rhythm – **r**hythm **h**elps **y**our **t**wo **h**ips **m**ove

- Break it into prefixes, root words, suffixes. *Example:* un-fortunate-ly

- Break it into syllables. *Examples:* re-mem-ber, beau-ti-ful

- Find a word within a word. *Examples:* fav-OUR-ite, sep-A-RAT-e

B

> **Homophones** are words that sound the same. They can be difficult to spell. You need to use strategies to help you learn them.

Words	Strategies
passed/ past	'Passed' is a verb: 'I passed my neighbour in the street.' 'Past' describes a previous point in time: 'I walked past the puppy.' You can remember it because 'past' has a 't' in it, for 'time'.
practice/ practise	'Practice' is a noun: 'I go to drum practice.' 'Practise' is a verb: 'I'll practise my drumming.' You can remember it because 'ice' (in the word 'pract**ice**') is a noun.

Develop strategies for remembering the difference between the following sets of words.

> board/bored   threw/through   desert/dessert   their/there/they're
> thought/fought   allowed/aloud

Tricky spellings

accommodation   friend
actually   happened
argument   height
beautiful   necessary
beginning   queue
believe   remember
caught   rhythm
definite   separate
diary   shoulder
disappear   strength
disappoint   unfortunately
embarrass   weird
favourite

Remember: a cat **c**urled in a c-shape

- Look at the poet's use of structure and rhythm
- Explore language and figurative techniques

Celebration

I shall dance tonight
When the dusk comes crawling
There will be dancing
and feasting.
5 I shall dance with the others
    in circles,
      in leaps,
        in stomps.
Laughter and talk
10 Will weave into night,
Among the fires
Of my people.
Games will be played
And I shall be
15 a part of it.

Alonzo Lopez

Comprehension

 1 What effect does the writer of *Celebration* create when he writes 'in circles, in leaps, in stomps' on separate lines?

2 In what other way does the writer create this effect?

3 What figurative language techniques have been used here?

- 'the dusk comes crawling'
- 'laughter and talk will weave into night'

4 What image does the writer create when he uses this figurative language?

5 What is the mood of the poem?

- Identify the mood in a poem
- Give an opinion on the poems

Sunbeam

I pray to the sunbeam from the window –
It is pale, thin, straight.
Since morning I have been silent,
And my heart – is split.
The copper on my washstand
Has turned green,
But the sunbeam plays on it
So charmingly.
How innocent it is, and simple,
In the evening calm,
But to me in this deserted temple
It's like a golden celebration,
And a consolation.

Anna Akhmatova

B 1 What clue is there that the poem *Sunbeam* was written a long time ago?

2 At what time of day is the poem set?

3 What is described as both a celebration and a comfort to the writer?

4 What sort of mood is the writer in? Why?

5 What effect do the dashes create in the first and fourth lines?

6 What effect does the writer create by making the third and last sentences longer than the first and second?

C **What do you think?**

How is the mood in the poems different? How do the two different poems make you feel? Which one do you prefer? Why?

● Identify figurative language

Poetic devices

 A

1 In pairs, match the poetic devices with the correct definition and example.

2 Think of two more examples for each technique.

Poetic device	Definition	Example
metaphor	Gives an animal or object human characteristics (emotions, sensations, speech, physical movement).	The water was as clear as glass.
rhyme	The word makes the sound being described.	The frog sat on a log next to a dog.
alliteration	A word or phrase is used more than once for effect.	When the dusk comes crawling.
onomatopoeia	Similar sounds in words are repeated (usually at the end of lines of poetry or songs).	A wisp of wind whispered through the leaves.
simile	Describes something as if it were something else.	The frog jumped into the water. Plop!
repetition	The first letter or sound in closely connected words is repeated.	Millions of people were queuing up to get a signed copy of her latest book.
personification	Compares the similarities between two things using 'like' or 'as'.	The diamonds shone brightly in the night sky.
hyperbole	Exaggeration is used for effect.	The stars are twinkling, twinkling in the sky.

● Write examples of figurative language

Hyperbole is undoubtedly the most amazing language device ever invented! Hyperbole uses exaggeration for effect. It is a popular device used in poetry.

B 1 Read the poem below.

I love birthday parties!

A mountain of crunchy crisps,
a river of fizzy lemonade,
umpteen billion sticky biscuits,
every sandwich ever invented
a sponge cake the size of a house,
and gallons of chocolate ice cream.
By the time the party's over,
I'll be ready to POP like a balloon!

2 Which words are used for exaggeration?

3 What figurative technique is used in the last line?

4 Write a short poem using hyperbole to describe your favourite celebration.

C **Look at this sentence.**

The firework shrieked with jubilant joy, fizz, whizz, fizz, whizz and popped into a rainbow of colours as pretty as a picture.

Which poetic devices are used? Write your own sentence connected with celebrations. See how many poetic devices you can include. Look at the list of techniques on page 102 to help you. Can you use them all?

Celebrating nature

The Boab tree of North West Australia is a relative of the Baobab trees of Africa. These trees have huge trunks and often have hollows, like huge caves, inside them.

The week-long Boab Festival starts at the end of July each year when its flower, the wattle, blooms.

Tree Festival

On the landscapes of Australia
  the weirdest shapes appear,
    so many **freaks of nature**
    that only **flourish** here.
5 There's one found in the north-west,
  no odder sight you'll see:
    a **relic** of the **Dreamtime**
    is the mighty Boab tree.
Out near the Fitroy River
10 a grim old tale they tell,
  how one great hollow Boab
  became a prison cell.
But now, when **wattle's** blooming,
  each year the people **throng**
15 to join the Boab Festival,
  for sport and dance and song,
And some will hold their picnics
  near a tribe's **Corroboree** –
  it's like a kind of **tribute**
20 to the mighty Boab tree.

David Bateson

- Choose a form for your poem
- Write it using figurative language and senses
- Perform the poem

Model writing

The 'Tree Festival' is held next to an Indigenous Australian site. Indigenous Australians lived in Australia long before the British arrived in the 18th century. The festival is a celebration of nature, history and culture.

Your writing

Write a poem, like 'Tree Festival', about a place near where you live (such as a park, forest, desert, river, lake or mountain) that you think would be a good place to hold a new festival or celebration.

- Where will the festival be?
- What will it celebrate?
- What time of year will it be held?

Writing frame

Setting	What picture will your poem create in the minds of your audience?
Use your senses	Consider what you might see, hear or smell in your poem – how will you convey this to your audience?
Details and objects	When you describe objects, use detail to create a vivid image.
Language	Use words you like, and consider how they sound. Think about synonyms and figurative language. What different techniques will you use? Have fun with words!
Style	There are many different forms and types of poems: narrative, sonnet, kenning, shape, etc. Choose your own form.

Presentation and performance

Read your poem and check for any errors.

When you have your final version of the poem, prepare a version that can be displayed in class.

Read your poem out loud. Consider how the punctuation and figurative language will be effective in a performance.

Rehearse your poem, then perform it for the class.

Revise and check (2)

Vocabulary

1 **Match the verbs to the following definitions.**

> flatter   stomp   leap   prance   flourish   crawl   nourish

  a to feed something   **e** to walk with big, heavy movements

  b to praise   **f** to move in a happy or lively way

  c to move on hands and knees   **g** to jump high in the air

  d to do really well

2 **Look at this sentence.**

The ant sat on it and floated to the riverbank safely.

Can you identify the word class of each word in the sentence?

3 **Choose the correct linking word to complete each sentence.**

> despite   yet   therefore   although   even though

_____ many parents agree that phones can be distracting, they do like to be able to contact their children. _____, head teachers are reluctant to ban them completely, _____ they affect school performance negatively.

Children are told to keep phones off in class, _____ 72% were found to ignore this rule. It was even discovered that, _____ knowing their children were in class, many parents have phoned their children.

4 **Write a more powerful synonym for each word below.**

> sad   happy   angry   ran   shout

Punctuation

1 **Explain why brackets have been used in this sentence.**

We think (and you know we're right) our product is the best on the market.

2 Add the commas to this sentence.

Our chocolate which has a glass of milk in every bar uses the finest cacao beans.

3 Write out these sentences using the correct punctuation from the list.

> commas   brackets   colon

a   The Vietnamese festival Trung Thu is celebrated in autumn.

b   Here is an example path sounds like bath.

c   The young very small skater whirled around the rink.

Grammar

1 Add the correct relative pronouns to the following sentences.

a   The man ——————— drives the yellow car is the owner of the company ——————— makes bicycles.

b   Mrs Ferrari is the woman ——————— ran the race in 6 minutes, ——————— is a new record!

c   I'd like to talk to the man, ——————— daughter won the tennis match.

Poetic devices

1 Say which techniques have been used in the following sentences.

> onomatopoeia   metaphor   hyperbole   rhyme
> personification   alliteration   simile

a   I'm going to freeze to death if you don't turn the heating up.

b   That little dog is as fast as a bullet.

c   The beastly black bug bit a big brown bear.

d   *Whoosh, bang, whoosh, bang* … back and forth went the tennis ball.

e   The chair stubbornly refused to budge an inch.

f   Grandma is a sturdy, old tree, with gnarled branches for fingers.

g   A blue moon in the month of June.

Spelling

1 Write four words with four different spellings of the /k/ sound.

7 Spies and mystery

Alex Rider, a teenage spy and hero of many adventures, such as in the film, *Stormbreaker*.

The *Spy Kids* films are popular all over the world.

"Every man is surrounded by a neighbourhood of voluntary spies."

Jane Austen

Talk time

1 A spy wears a disguise so they are not recognised. If you were a spy, what would you change about how you look, move and speak so that no one knew it was you?

2 What genre do you think the Alex Rider spy books belong to?

- Discuss narrative genres
- State your genre preferences

Spy words uncovered

A Here are some words found in spy books and films.
Match the words below with the correct definitions (1–7).

Example: spymaster 7

> bug   code   intelligence   secret agent   spymaster   surveillance   alias

Definitions

1 Useful information
2 A hidden microphone which records conversation
3 Watching someone over a period of time
4 Another term for a spy
5 A false name and identity
6 Letters, numbers and symbols used to send hidden messages
7 A person who controls several spies

B Fill in the blanks with some of the words and phrases above.

I am a _____ and my _____ is _____ [you decide what your 'spy name' is]. I sometimes hide an electronic _____ to record what people are saying. When I need to send a message, I use _____. I pretend that I am an estate agent, which means that I can carry out _____ and nobody is suspicious.

C **What about you?**

Discuss these questions with your partner.

Have you read any of the Alex Rider books or any other spy thrillers? Do you like reading the spy thriller genre? Why/Why not? Can you recommend any good spy thrillers for your partner to read?

Narrative voice and viewpoint

A Read the opening two paragraphs from *Young Bond: Double or Die* and answer the questions.

Young Bond

James was filled with a burning excitement. He needed the thrill of danger. It was only on an adventure like this that he came alive. His day-to-day life at school felt grey and dull, but now the boredom had lifted and all his senses were heightened.

5 That didn't mean he could be careless, however. The goggles, hats and scarves were as much worn as disguises as to shield the two boys from the cutting wind. They were speeding away from Eton towards Cambridge having left a pack of lies behind them. A pack of lies that could soon be snapping at their heels

10 if they didn't watch out.

James thought back to when this had begun. It had been the end of the summer holidays, a few days before James was due to return to Eton. He had been helping out at the Duck Inn in Pett Bottom, the village where he lived with his Aunt

15 Charmian… He was rolling an empty barrel across the ground when he looked up from his work and saw a black car driving through the fields. He straightened up and followed its progress. There was a chill in the air and he shivered.

From *Young Bond: Double or Die* by Charlie Higson

1 Is this narrative told in first person, second person or third person? How do you know? Who is telling the story?

2 From whose point of view is the story being told? How do you know?

3 Who says 'A pack of lies that could soon be snapping at their heels…'? What does this tell us about the storyteller?

4 Why does the writer start the story with James and his companion speeding to Cambridge, rather that starting at the beginning?

5 Find the sentence which introduces the flashback to what's happened before the story starts.

6 What effect does the last sentence have?

In fiction books, there are usually two types of **narrative voice**: first person (see *Kara's one big chance* [page 10]/*Going Hunting* [page 14]) or third person (*Young Bond: Double or Die* [page 110]). It is possible to use second person (you/your), but few writers choose to write a story in second person.

First person

1   The protagonist

The story is told by the protagonist – the main character. The reader knows all their thoughts, opinions and feelings, which means we get to know the main character faster, and relate to them more easily. Some of the main pronouns used are: *I, my, me, we*.

Third person

2   The detached narrator

A detached third person narrator tells the story without giving any of their own opinions. You probably won't notice their voice at all. The main pronouns used are: *she, he* and *they*.

3   The omniscient narrator

This narrator is all-knowing (omniscient), so they know everyone's thoughts and what will happen before events are told. The main pronouns used are *she, he* and *they*. Foreboding comments are sometimes used, such as: 'If only she'd known, she'd never have…'

B **1** Below is the same event in a story being told from different viewpoints. Match the examples below with one of the viewpoints described above.

  a 'I can't believe I'm doing this!' I thought, as I sprinted as fast as I could for the cover of the trees. 'I'm not going to make it!'

  b James was convinced he wasn't going to make it, but he sprinted as fast as he could for the cover of the trees. Little did he know what awaited him in the woods…

  c James ran for the cover of the trees as fast as he could.

  2 Write an example of your own for each of the viewpoints.

C **What are the advantages and disadvantages of telling a story from a detached narrator's point of view? Are there more advantages from telling a story using an omniscient narrator?**

- Look at story openings
- Recognise a narrative voice

Story beginnings

Read the opening two paragraphs from *Stormbreaker*.

How it all began

When the doorbell rings at three in the morning, it's never good news. Alex Rider was woken by the first **chime**. His eyes flicked open but for a moment he stayed completely still in his bed, lying on his back with his head resting on
5 a pillow. He heard a bedroom door open and a creak of wood as somebody went downstairs. The bell rang a second time and he looked at his alarm clock glowing beside him. 3.02 a.m. There was a rattle as someone slid the security chain off the front door.

10 He rolled out of bed and walked over to the main window, his bare feet pressing down the carpet pile. The moonlight spilled on to his chest and shoulders. Alex was fourteen, already well-built, with the body of an athlete. His hair, cut short apart from two thick strands hanging over his
15 forehead, was fair. His eyes were brown and serious. For a moment he stood silently, half hidden in the shadow, looking out.

From *Stormbreaker* by Anthony Horowitz

A Discuss these questions with your partner.

1 Is the text a first or third person narrative?

2 What kind of narrative viewpoint is the story told in?

3 Look at the first line. Who is saying or thinking this? What effect does the opening line have on the reader?

4 How is the order of events in these paragraphs different to the order in the opening paragraphs of the *Young Bond* text? (page 110)

5 Which opening do you prefer? Why?

 Stretch zone

Find the opening paragraphs to other thrillers. How does the writer grab the reader's attention and make them want to read on?

- Explore word origins
- Look at prefixes and suffixes

The origins of words

The English language that we use today has many different origins. Words have come from different countries. For example, the word **spy** comes from the 13th century old French word **espier** which means 'one who spies on another'.

A Many words are formed around Latin roots. Find the Latin root in each of the words below. Use the table of meanings to help you.

chilli con carne	sensitive	vitamin	carnivorous
annual	anniversary	vitality	sensible

Latin root	Meaning
ann	year
carn	meat
sens	feel, be aware
vit	life

Stretch zone

Using an online dictionary, find out where these words came from: **clue, cafe, alphabet, algebra, cup**.

B The same roots, prefixes and suffixes are used in lots of words. Think of two words to add to this word web using the same prefix: tele– and the suffix: –ible.

television

tele———

visible

———ible

C Throughout history, the English language has borrowed many words from other languages, through travel, exploration or even war. Read the words that come from each of these countries in the table below.

Country	Word
Mexico	tomato
Greece	theatre, marathon
Italy	piano, umbrella
Turkey	coffee, yoghurt, sofa

Mystery and suspense

Alex Rider's uncle was mysteriously killed. Alex discovers he was a spy and is asked to continue his uncle's mission to stop the villain, Herod Sayle, giving free but dangerous 'Stormbreaker' computers to all schools. But Alex doesn't want to be a spy…

Alex becomes a spy

"Who are you?" Alex asked. "What do you want with me?"

"My name is Blunt. I am Chief Executive of the Special Operations Division of **MI6**. Mrs Jones here is our Head of Special Operations. She gave your uncle his last **assignment**," he replied…

5 "What we're suggesting is that you come and work for us," Mrs Jones said. "We have enough time to give you some basic training – not that you'll need it, probably. You'll be able to meet Herod Sayle, keep an eye on him, and tell us what you think. Perhaps you'll also find out what it was that your uncle discovered and
10 why he had to die. You shouldn't be in any danger. After all, who would suspect a fourteen-year-old boy of being a spy?"

"All we're asking you to do is to report back to us," Blunt said. "That's all we want. Two weeks of your time. A chance to make sure these computers are everything they're cracked up to be.
15 A chance to serve your country."

"No," Alex said.

"I'm sorry?"

"It's a dumb idea. I don't want to be a spy. I want to be a footballer. Anyway, I have a life of my own!" He found it
20 difficult to choose the right words. The whole thing was so **preposterous** he almost wanted to laugh. "Why don't you ask this Felix Lester to **snoop** around for you?"

"We don't believe he'd be as **resourceful** as you," Blunt said.

- Discuss the writer's language
- Examine character

25 "He's probably better at computer games." Alex shook his head. "I'm sorry. I'm just not interested. I don't want to get involved."

"That's a pity," Blunt said. "Then we'd better move on to discuss your future," he continued. "Ian Rider has of course left the house and all his money to you. However, 30 he left it in **trust** until you are twenty-one. And we control that trust."

"You're **blackmailing** me!" Alex exclaimed.

"Not at all."

"But if I agree to do what you ask... ?"

35 Blunt glanced at Mrs Jones. "Help us and we'll help you," she said.

From *Stormbreaker* by Anthony Horowitz

Glossary

MI6 Secret Intelligence Service in the UK

assignment job or task

preposterous ridiculous

snoop look around secretly

resourceful quick and clever, especially in a difficult situation

trust a person holds money or property for another person

blackmailing threaten someone to make them do what you want

Comprehension

A Listen and respond

1 Who are Blunt and Mrs Jones?

2 What do they want Alex to do?

3 How many weeks of Alex's time do they want?

B Read and respond

1 Why is an ellipsis used on line 4?

2 What exactly do Blunt and Mrs Jones want Alex to do?

3 Look at lines 18–19. Why does Alex repeat 'I' three times?

4 Blunt uses different methods to persuade Alex to become a spy. Find evidence from the text to match the three methods below.

   a Blunt appeals to Alex's loyalty to his country.

   b Blunt flatters Alex.

   c Blunt blackmails him.

C What do you think?

1 Why is Herod Sayle giving free computers out to schools? What do you think his aim is?

2 Would you accept the job if you were Alex? Why/Why not? What do you think Alex will do?

3 Is this the sort of book you'd like to read? Why/Why not?

- Compare narratives and graphic novels
- Create a graphic novel

Read the page from the graphic novel and answer the questions.

A

1 Mr Blunt uses a different method here to try to convince Alex to change his mind. What does he do?

2 Look at the second box. Why is an ellipsis used?

3 Why do the shape of Alex's speech bubbles change at the end?

B

1 Look at how the dialogue is presented differently in the narrative text (pages 114–115) and graphic novel.

2 Explain to your partner what the rules are for writing dialogue in a narrative and then say how this differs in a graphic novel.

C **What do you think?**

1 What do you think Blunt shows Alex to convince him to be a spy? Do you think it has something to do with his uncle?

2 Do you read any graphic novels? Do you prefer reading narrative books or graphic novels?

3 Divide the story extract on pages 114–115 into six scenes. Divide an A4 piece of paper into six shapes – they don't have to all be square boxes (look at the shapes in the graphic novel). You will be telling the same story, but this time through drawing and using speech bubbles for dialogue. You may need to leave out some information.

This page from the graphic novel of *Stormbreaker* is also about Alex becoming a spy.

● Understand idioms and proverbs

Proverbs and idioms

The extract 'Alex becomes a spy' contains some **idioms**. *Examples:* 'keep an eye on him' (watch him) and 'everything they're cracked up to be' (as good as they're meant to be). An idiom is an expression where the actual meaning is different from the literal meaning.

 A 1 Complete these popular idioms with a word from the list below. Use the meanings to help you.

hat   tree   thoughts

a   At the drop of a _____. (straight away, immediately)

b   A penny for your _____ . (What are you thinking?)

c   Barking up the wrong _____. (making a mistake)

2 Idioms are used when people are speaking informally. Match the idioms (a–c) to the correct phrases (1–3).

a on the tip of my tongue	1 get to the point
b from scratch	2 from the beginning
c cut a long story short	3 you know the word, but can't remember it

A **proverb** is an expression that gives advice.

Example: 'All that glitters is not gold' means things aren't always as valuable as they might seem.

B Read these three proverbs from different countries. Choose one that you like. Write it out and draw an illustration to show what it means.

China: A journey of a thousand miles begins with a single step.

Egypt: A beautiful thing is never perfect. (Something can be beautiful but not perfect.)

Finland: Even a small star shines in the darkness. (Everything has its worth.)

Active and passive voice

Reasons for using the passive voice

In Standard English, it is more common to use the **active voice** because forming the passive makes the information longer and it can seem awkward. Sometimes though, writers choose to use the **passive voice** for the following reasons:

- To make the tone more formal. *Example:* Any unauthorised people entering the building will be detained.

- Because the subject is not known. *Example:* Graffiti has been sprayed all over the school gates!

- To take the emphasis away from the subject because it is not as important as the object. *Example:* A million pounds will be given to the lucky winner.

- To make a narrative more exciting. *Example:* He was being watched by someone … or something!

A **1** Say which sentence in each pair is in the passive voice.

    a Heavy rain flattened all the plants.

       All the plants were flattened by heavy rain.

    b The missing parrot has been found by Anton.

       Anton has found the missing parrot.

    c The front of the school is hidden by trees.

       Trees hide the front of the school.

    d Sandhya will bring the children home.

       The children will be brought home by Sandhya.

2 What are the rules for turning an active sentence into a passive one?

- Identify active and passive voice

B **Decide whether the following sentences are in the active or passive voice. Then change them into the opposite voice.**

1 The headmaster closed the school for the summer yesterday.

2 The back door is left open by me so the cat can come in and out.

3 We'll be called by my mum for dinner soon.

4 Dad is making us a delicious spicy curry.

5 Pavol's grandmother was visited by friends yesterday.

C 1 Copy and complete the sentences by writing the passive form of the verb in brackets.

a Li Wei and Li Jing __________ (take) to school this morning by their big brother.

b The new sports centre __________ (open) next month by Cristiano Ronaldo.

c At this moment, I can hear a violin __________ (play) in the music room.

d The horses __________ (feed) twice a day, every day.

e He was finally able to the buy the new game because he __________ (give) some money for his birthday.

2 Write three more passive sentences which each have a different verb form.

Language tips

The passive voice is when the subject of the sentence has something done to it by someone or something. *For example:* The mouse was being chased by the cat.

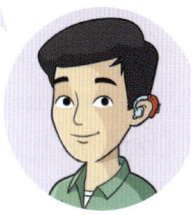

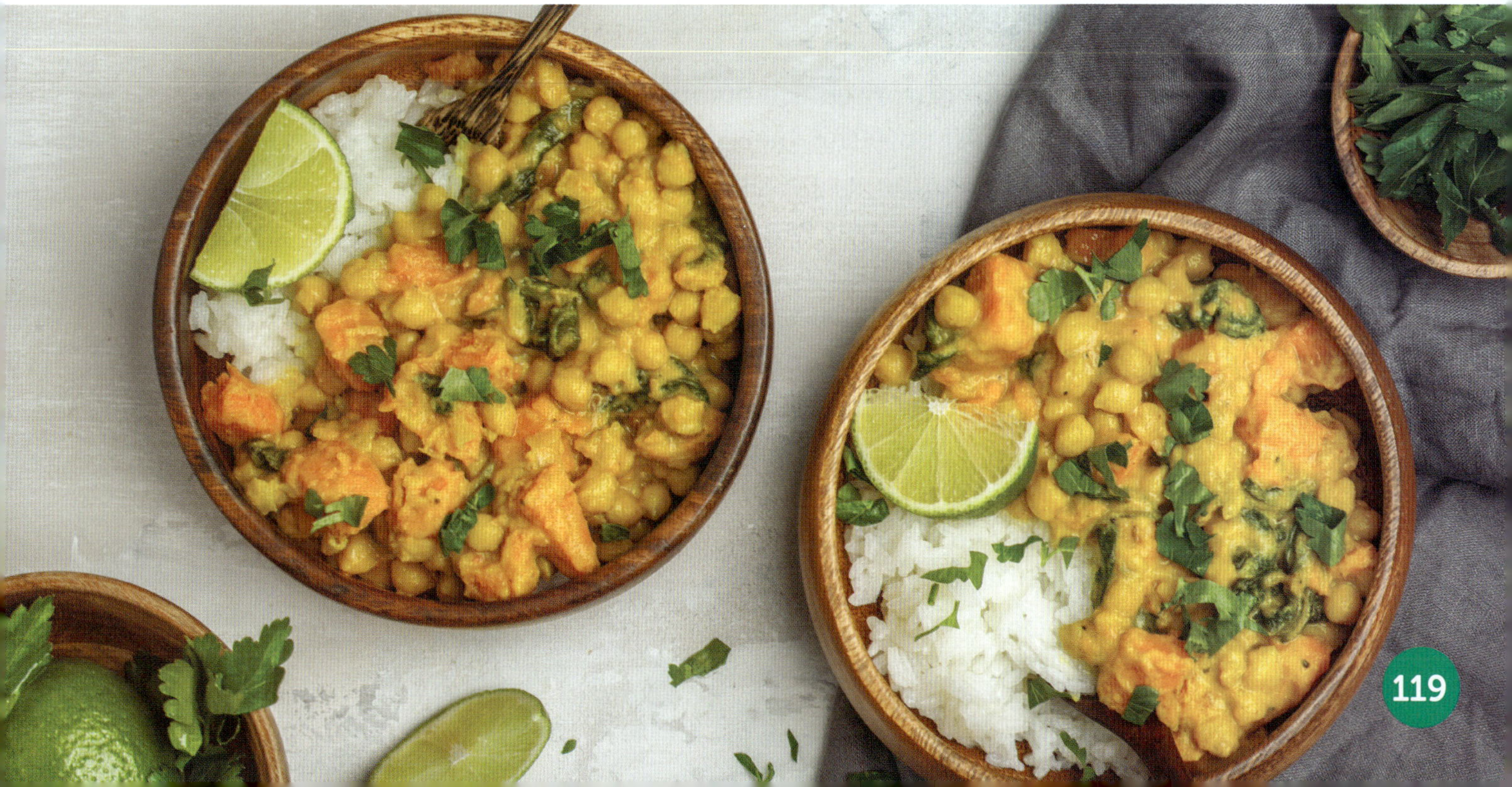

This story takes place in a small village in north Botswana. A father, Obed, is telling his daughter, Precious, the story of when he came face to face with a lion.

Botswana's greatest detective

I looked up at the night sky and thought, 'I'll never see the sun again.' But the next thing I said to myself was, 'No, I must do something. I must not let this lion eat me!'

"I made up my mind and ran – not back to the hut, but to
5 the nearest <u>grain</u> bin. I pushed the cover back and jumped in, bringing the lid down on top of my head. I was safe!"

Precious breathed a sigh of relief. But she knew that there was more to come.

"There was very little grain left in that bin," Obed went
10 on. "There were just a few husks and dusty bits. So there was plenty of room for me to crouch down...

"The lion had been a bit surprised when I jumped into the bin, and now I could hear him outside, scratching and <u>snuffling</u> at the lid. I knew that it would only be a matter of
15 time before he pushed the lid off with one of his great paws, and I knew that I had to do something. But what could I do?"

Precious knew the answer. "You could take some of the dusty bits and pieces from the bottom of the bin and..."

Obed laughed. "Exactly. And that's what I did. I took
20 a handful of those dusty <u>husks</u> and then, pushing up the lid a tiny bit, I <u>tossed</u> them straight into the face of the <u>inquisitive</u> lion..."

Obed smiled. "He was very surprised. He breathed in then gave the loudest, most powerful sneeze that
25 has ever been sneezed in Botswana, or possibly in all of Africa... It was a sneeze that was heard by everybody in the village. In every hut, people awoke, rubbed their eyes, and rose from their sleeping mats. 'A great lion has sneezed,' they said to one another.
30 'We must all hit pots and pans as hard as we can. That will frighten him away.' And that's what happened..."

"I am glad you were not eaten by that lion," said Precious.

35 "And so am I," said Obed.

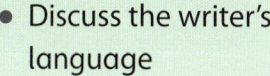

- Discuss the writer's language
- Understand words in context

"Because if the lion had eaten you, I would never have been born."

"And if you had never been born, then I would never have been able to get to know the brightest and nicest girl in all
40 Botswana," said her father.

Precious thought for a moment. "So it would have been a bad thing for both of us," she said at last.

"Yes," said Obed. "And maybe a bad thing for the lion too."

"Oh, why was that?"

45 "Because I might have given him <u>indigestion</u>," said Obed. "It's a well-known fact that if a lion eats a person who's feeling cross at the time, he gets indigestion."

Precious looked at her father <u>suspiciously</u>. She was not sure whether this was true, or whether he was just making it up to amuse her. She decided it
50 was not true and told him so.

He smiled and looked at her in a curious way. "You can tell when people are making things up, can't you? Perhaps you should become a detective one day," he said.

And that was how the idea of becoming a detective was first planted in
55 the mind of Precious Ramotswe, who was still only seven, but who was about to embark on a career as Botswana's greatest detective!

From *Precious and the Monkeys: Precious Ramotswe's Very First Case* by Alexander McCall Smith

Comprehension

A **Listen and respond**

1 Where did Obed hide from the lion?

2 Has Precious heard this story before? How do you know?

B **Read and respond**

1 Why doesn't the lion attack Obed before he jumps into the bin?

2 Was Obed safe in the grain bin? Explain your answer.

3 How did the villagers frighten the lion away?

4 What gives Precious the idea to become a detective?

C Match the words underlined in the text with the correct definition below. Try to use the context to work out the meaning. Then use a dictionary to check your answers.

1 threw   2 without trust   3 pain after eating food   4 wheat or other farmed cereal
5 sniffing   6 curious   7 dry covering of a grain

Handling of time

- Understand the order of events
- Understand non-chronological order
- Use adverbials of time to sequence

Obed tells the story of the lion in chronological order. That is, he tells the events of the story in the order they happen. In a narrative, events can be described in chronological order or they can be told out of the order in which they happened. This can add mystery and excitement to a story.

Example: You could start a story with: 'I edged the lid open a crack so I could see out and looked straight into the fierce brown eyes of the lion.' The reader would be hooked and want to know more. The writer could then go back in time to explain why they were hiding in a grain bin and why a lion was looking for them.

A Look at this picture of Obed hiding in the grain bin. Retell the story as if you are Obed. This time, however, start the story at the point when you are hiding in the grain bin. Describe the events that happened before you hid in the bin to explain why you are there, then carry on to explain how it ended.

Use some of the adverbials of time in the box below to help you sequence your story.

> after a while   at once   at this point   finally   first   in the end
> later on   meanwhile   next   next time   now   previously   since
> soon   then   when   whenever   while

B Read the extract *Young Bond: Double or Die* on page 110 again. Draw a timeline like the one below. Then put the following events (a–e) on the timeline in chronological order. The first one has been done for you.

   a James telling a lot of lies to people in Eton

   b James driving with a friend to Cambridge

   c James returning to Eton after the summer holidays

   d James working at an inn in his aunt's village

   e James seeing a black car approaching

d

- Discuss the action thriller genre
- Look at effective openings

Third person narrative: An action thriller

Story openers

You are going to write an action thriller using third person narrative.

1   First, think of an exciting opening for your story.

Stormbreaker begins like this:

'When the doorbell rings at three in the morning, it is never good news.'

Young Bond: Double or Die begins:

'The pistol was a six-shot revolver with a short, stubby barrel. Not very accurate at long range, but deadly enough close up.'

Here are four more examples of story openings. Choose the one you like best, or use an opening of your own.

1 Her phone was buzzing. Who could be calling her at 3 o'clock in the morning?	**2** He heard the soft squeal of a car's tyres behind him and walked faster. Were they onto him already?
3 He heard the key turn in the lock and realised he was completely trapped inside.	**4** Lucy got into the car quickly. She turned to thank the driver. And that's when she saw who it was...

Now make some notes to help you write your own action thriller.

- Use a plan to make notes

2   Copy the plan below and use the table to write notes for a narrative of six or more paragraphs.

Topic	Notes
The hero/heroine: You can make yourself the hero/heroine but you need to describe yourself in third person, NOT first person. *Example:* She had a large mop of straw-coloured hair and soft, brown eyes.	
The villain: What do they look like? How do they speak? Is there anything distinctive about their character or appearance?	
Setting: Choose somewhere that you are familiar with – that way you can give lots of descriptive detail. Don't just describe what you can see; use your other senses too and describe what you can hear, smell, feel and even taste.	
The mystery: What's the mystery? A disappearing friend, pet, family member? Strange night-time events in your town, at your neighbour's house, at school? Receiving a mysterious parcel from a stranger?	
Using cliffhangers: Try to end your paragraphs on cliffhangers. For example, your character might be alone in a dangerous place, come face to face with the villain, be trapped somewhere, or about to be hurt by someone or something.	
Building up tension: Does your character get into trouble? Were they found out? Is a villain hot on their trail? Does the mystery event happen again? For example, does another friend disappear? Does another mysterious parcel arrive?	
Resolving the mystery: How does it all end? Does your character save the day, save someone, save the world, solve the mystery that no one else could, reveal something surprising that nobody else knew?	

- Give and receive feedback
- Write a story opening
- Edit your work

3 When you have completed your notes, share your story opener and plan with your partner. Give feedback to each other. Are the events in the story clear and logical? Is the story exciting? Does the excitement build up to a dramatic ending? Can you think of anything that would make the story even better?

4 Use your paragraph notes, your partner's feedback and the list of action thriller success criteria below to help you write your action thriller narrative. Check and edit your story as you write. When you have finished writing, swap stories with a new partner. Use the success criteria to edit your partner's story. Give your partner feedback.

Action thriller success criteria

There is an exciting opening.

The story develops logically.

There's a build-up of tension, with powerful verbs used.

A mixture of sentence types and length make the narrative interesting and build up tension.

Characters are shown by what they say, how they move and how they behave.

Settings are well-described and realistic.

Third person perspective is consistently used.

The past tense is used consistently.

The correct spelling, punctuation and grammar is used throughout the story.

Language tip

- Use powerful verbs like snarl, growl, whisper, bellow.
- Use strong, realistic dialogue: "Look out! He's behind you!"
- Use similes and adjectives: 'He looked like a wrinkled toad.'
- Move your story on by using adverbials of time such as: later, after.

5 Share your story with the class. Remember to bring your characters to life and make the story more exciting by using different voices and facial expressions as you read.

8 Conserving our precious planet

A

B

C

D

"Judge a man by his questions rather than by his answers."

Voltaire, 1694–1778

Talk time

1 Why do you think it is important to find out about our world?

2 Why do you think it is important to protect our planet and the environment for future generations?

126

Discovering and protecting our precious world

- Match captions and pictures
- Explore the word ending -ist

A Match the captions (1–6) to the photos and drawings (A–F) on pages 126 and 127.

Example: **1 = E**

1 Hippocrates, an ancient Greek doctor, discovered that the bark and leaves of the willow tree cured headaches and fevers.

2 Artists who travelled with Joseph Banks, the explorer and scientist, drew pictures of plants like this breadfruit.

3 Many modern medicines are produced from plants found in tropical rainforests.

4 With only about 63 Māui dolphins left in the wild, they are top of the list of **critically endangered** animals.

5 This drawing shows that Mexicans collected **medicinal** plants.

6 Divers are making exciting discoveries about a lost underwater city in Egypt.

> **Glossary**
>
> **critically endangered** threatened or at risk of extinction
> **medicinal** helping to cure an illness

B These people all study, discover or protect things. Talk about them and match the words and explanations. Which one would you like to be?

archaeologist	studies the protection of the environment and wildlife
conservationist	studies plants
marine archaeologist	studies rocks
zoologist	studies things from the past that have been discovered underwater
botanist	studies animals and birds
geologist	studies history by examining things from the past

E

F

The Galápagos Islands

Expedition of a lifetime

I couldn't believe my ears when I got the phone call to say that I was on my way to the Galápagos Islands! I won the trip by entering a photo competition in a wildlife magazine.

5 Three months later, we were flying over the Galápagos Islands towards Seymour Airport. What a beautiful sight! The islands lie about 1,000 kilometres off the coast of Ecuador, in the Eastern Pacific Ocean. There

10 are about 13 large islands and 6 smaller ones, with a population of approximately 25,000. The islands are like nowhere else in the world. Because of their **isolation**, **unique species** developed without any

15 humans interfering over thousands of years.

Protected species

Our first stop was the Charles Darwin Research Station to see the giant tortoises and hear about the island's **conservation**

20 programmes. The tortoises live a slow-paced life, and so would you if you weighed 250 kilograms! They eat leaves and grass, and sleep for up to 16 hours a day. They commonly live to over 100 years,

25 and the record is 175 years. When Darwin visited in 1835, there were 15 species of tortoise, but now there are only 10 left.

Vegetarian monsters

In the afternoon, we walked down to the

30 beach in search of **marine** iguanas. Here's a photo of one that I took. It looks incredibly fierce and prehistoric, like a dinosaur, but in fact they are harmless and live off seaweed. When they come onto dry

35 land, they line up with their heads facing the wind and sneeze to get rid of the salt that they have breathed in.

A mate for life

On our last day, we visited a protected

40 **breeding** site for the waved **albatross** on the island of Española. Our guide told us some fascinating facts about the only tropical albatross in the world. They have a huge **wingspan** of over two metres and

45 mate for life. We saw some of the scruffy-looking chicks through binoculars. They grow into graceful adults which are very good at flying. When they leave the nest, they spend the next six years at sea off the

50 coast of Peru, eventually returning to the islands to breed.

A life-changing experience

We left after an amazing ten days on the islands. Not only was it the most incredible

55 trip of my life, but it got me interested in conservation programmes, so I think that from now on my life will take a different course.

Glossary

isolation being away from everything
unique species the only type of an animal or bird
conservation looking after the natural environmen[t]
marine sea
breeding mating and production of baby animals/birds
albatross large seabird
wingspan measurement from the tip of one wing to the tip of the other

Comprehension

A **Listen and respond**

1 Why are the animals on the Galápagos Islands so special?

2 What reason does the writer give for the tortoises being so slow?

3 Why do the iguanas face their heads to the wind?

4 What is unique about the albatrosses on the island?

B **Read and respond**

1 How does the writer feel when they receive the phone call?

2 What does the writer think of their first glimpse of the Galápagos Islands?

3 What are the writer's impressions of the marine iguana, and the albatross chicks?

4 Give one phrase from the text that tells us how the writer felt about the whole experience of going to the Galápagos.

5 The writer uses adverbials of time such as 'three months later' to structure the text. Find two more adverbials of time.

C **What do you think?**

Use information from the text to support your answers.

1 Why do you think the writer's experience on the islands led them to become interested in conservation?

2 Do you think it is important to save the animals on the islands from extinction?

3 Should tourists be allowed to visit the islands?

4 Explain in your own words what makes the Galápagos Islands so special.

Giant tortoise

Baby albatross

Adult albatross

? Your local community has asked students to recommend a local animal that they can help to protect. Which animal would you choose and why?

Using imperative verbs

We use an **imperative verb** at the beginning of a sentence to:
- Write a command. *Examples:* **shut** the gate, **keep off** the grass
- Write an instruction. *Example:* **chop** the onion finely

Starting a sentence with the imperative verb makes the command or instruction very clear. A list of instructions (such as a recipe) describes how something is done step by step.

A Look at the instructions for making a mini rainforest. Complete the sentences using an imperative verb from the list below.

Spray   Screw   Plant   Put   Add   Place   Wet   Watch

1 _____ the gravel and charcoal in the bottom of the glass jar.

2 _____ the soil in a layer of at least 4 cm on top of the gravel and charcoal.

3 _____ the soil slightly.

4 _____ the plants in the jar carefully, so you don't damage them.

5 _____ water inside the jar with a spray bottle.

6 _____ on the lid. If you like, you can put tape around the edges to seal it.

7 _____ your glass jar in a warm, well-lit spot.

8 _____ what happens – keep a notebook.

B Complete the instructions above by adding the list of materials needed to make the rainforest. Use the heading 'You will need:'

C Think of suitable imperative verbs to complete these instructions to make a tropical fruit smoothie. Here are a few ideas to help you: peel, chop, squeeze.

Ingredients: a pineapple, ½ a banana, an orange, coconut milk, a lime, vanilla yogurt, ice cubes.

First, _____ the pineapple and _____ into small chunks. _____ in a blender. Next, _____ the orange and the lime, then _____ their juice into the blender with the pineapple. _____ all the remaining ingredients. _____ the mixture until smooth. _____ immediately and enjoy!

- Use imperatives in instructions
- Use adverbials of time to sequence

More imperatives and adverbials of time

A Match the imperative verbs (1–6) to the correct command or instruction (a–f).

1	stick	**a**	off the grass
2	melt	**b**	the butter and pour into the dish
3	fold	**c**	at your own risk
4	drive	**d**	carefully
5	keep	**e**	along the dotted line
6	enter	**f**	the shapes on with glue

Some lists of instructions are sequenced by numbers. Others use **adverbials of time** before the imperative verb. These include: first, then, next, after that, meanwhile, as, before, while, afterwards, finally.

B Use the pictures below to write a list of instructions for how to draw a parrot. Use a different adverbial of time to introduce the instructions for each new drawing.

Here are some adverbials of time you can choose from:

before   as soon as   after   that   next   once   when   first

Example: First, draw a circle for the head of the parrot and an oval just below it for the body.

When you have finished writing your instructions, add a suitable heading and a list of the materials you will need.

Stretch zone

Choose a task that you do regularly, like brushing your teeth, or a recipe that you make a lot. Write step-by-step instructions for how to do it.

C Write a list of instructions describing how to get from your home to your school.

131

Last chance for Māui dolphins

Māui dolphins are a type of Hector's dolphin, the world's smallest dolphins. Māui dolphins are also one of the **rarest** dolphins, and can only be found on the west coast of the North Island of New Zealand. There are believed to be only 55–75 adult Māui dolphins left in the wild. They are on the edge of **extinction**. If action isn't taken now, we could lose them forever.

Human threats

Māui dolphins live very close to places where humans fish or sail boats. Occasionally they go into **harbours**, which can result in them becoming trapped in fishing nets. This is the largest cause of death of Māui dolphins by humans. Māui dolphins are also **vulnerable** to being hit by boats or their propellers.

Pollution is another major threat to all marine life, including the Māui dolphin. In particular, dolphins can become trapped in plastics, or they can eat them. It's up to us to minimise these threats to protect Māui dolphins for future **generations**.

Natural problems

Of course, not all threats of extinction come from humans – some threats are beyond our control. Māui dolphins have short lifespans compared to other dolphins and whales, and are slow to reproduce. Females have their first calf when they are 7–9 years of age. They produce just one calf every 2–4 years, meaning that they can only increase their population by 2% a year. As a result, a population of approximately 55 can only increase by 1 dolphin per year.

There is also the threat of disease and Māui dolphins being hunted by sharks and killer whales.

Time for action

It is still possible to save Māui dolphins. Big steps forward have been taken to help protect them. There has been a ban on using fishing nets along part of the North Island's west coast. But more must be done. Join our campaign to encourage people to use methods of fishing that are safe for dolphins.

These dolphins are on the very **brink** of extinction. With your help, we will save them!

Glossary

rarest most unusual, not found very often at all

extinction not existing any more

harbours places on the coast where ships stop

vulnerable in a position where something can be easily attacked or harmed

generations people born and living at about the same time

brink edge

Comprehension

- Understand the effect of language
- Identify emotive language

A Listen and respond

1 Where do Māui dolphins live?

2 Which two superlative forms are used to describe Māui dolphins in the first paragraph?

3 Why does the writer start a sentence with 'if' at the end of the first paragraph?

4 What are the different threats to the dolphins caused by humans?

5 Why is population growth of Māui dolphins slow? Give two reasons.

6 What is the name given to baby dolphins?

7 Which animals prey on the Māui dolphins?

In small groups, choose and plan a campaign for a real cause. Decide your action steps and then explain why this is such a good cause and your plan of action to the rest of the class.

B Read and respond

1 Look at the first paragraph. Which phrase tells us the information is not a certain fact?

2 List three features of non-chronological information reports found in this text.

3 Look at the last paragraph. What is the purpose of the campaign?

4 Which phrase in the text indicates that the writer is confident of success?

C What do you think?

1 Is it important for a country to protect their rare species of animals? Why/Why not?

2 Sometimes a species from another country will come to a country and wipe out a species which was already there. Does this matter or is it survival of the stronger species?

3 Is it our responsibility to try to save endangered animals or is it part of a natural process?

Stretch zone

Find out about threatened or endangered species indigenous to your country.

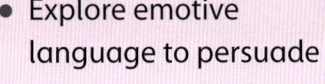

- Explore emotive language to persuade
- Use emotive language

Persuasive campaigns

In Unit 5, we looked at the techniques writers use to persuade their readers to do something. In 'Last chance for Māui dolphins', the writer chooses words and phrases to convince the reader that Māui dolphins must be saved from extinction immediately.

A Find phrases in the text which mean the same as the definitions below. The number of words and the section where you will find the phrase have been given. The first one has been done for you.

	Section	Number of words	Definition	Word/phrase from text
1	Last chance for Māui dolphins	5	if something isn't done immediately	if action isn't taken now
2	Human threats	3	reduce the harm that could be done	
3	Human threats	7	one more huge danger to all sea creatures	
4	Natural problems	3	nothing we can do about it	
5	Natural problems	2	don't live long	
6	Time for action	3	improvements	

B Find three emotive or dramatic words, phrases or sentences used in the text. Explain what impact they have on the reader.

C You have been asked to write a paragraph for the local newspaper on an animal that is soon going to be extinct. You must convince readers that something needs to be done. Use the following words and some more of your own choice.

> rarest   battle   extinct   survival   urgency

Red pandas are endangered.

Multi-clause sentences

Remember! A **multi-clause sentence** can consist of a main clause and one or more subordinate clauses. A **subordinating conjunction** is used to link clauses together.

Example: English is a popular subject, **although** it is difficult to learn. OR **Although** English is difficult to learn, it is a popular subject.

A Use a subordinating conjunction from the list below to join each pair of clauses into a multi-clause sentence. Use each conjunction only once.

while   because   although   until   when   after

1 it was cold and wet
we still went for a walk before school

2 gymnastics lessons will be stopped
too many children are scared of heights

3 we knew something was wrong
he didn't come to school

4 there are changes in students' behaviour
ballgames will be forbidden

5 Aida was eating her dinner
watching her favourite programme on TV

6 Ali and Saleem went to the cinema
they had been given their pocket money

B Write out the sentences from activity A. Decide if a comma is necessary and underline the subordinate clause. Try to vary the position of the subordinate clause.

C Write this paragraph out, using subordinating conjunctions and commas to complete the text.

Māui dolphins _____ are the smallest and the rarest dolphins in the world are only found off the coast of New Zealand's North Island. Recent studies show that _____ the dolphins are protected numbers are still declining. Māui and Hector's dolphins look identical _____ they are genetically different. Māui and Hector's dolphins look different to other dolphins _____ they have rounded fins _____ other dolphins usually have a pointed fin. Māui dolphins live up to 20 years _____ is a relatively short lifespan for a dolphin.

Conserving rainforests

Why are rainforests important?

Tropical rainforests are believed to be the oldest and most complex land-based <u>ecosystem</u> on earth, containing over 30 million species of plants and animals. That's half of the Earth's wildlife and at least two-thirds of its plant <u>species</u>! There are many more thousands of
5 rainforest plants and animals species still waiting to be discovered!

They regulate our climate

Rainforests store water like a huge sponge. In fact, it is believed that the Amazonian forests alone store over half of the Earth's rainwater! Rainforest trees draw water from the forest floor and release it back
10 in to the atmosphere in the form of swirling mists and clouds. Without rainforests continually recycling huge quantities of water, feeding the rivers, lakes and <u>irrigation</u> systems, <u>droughts</u> would become more common, potentially leading to widespread <u>famine</u> and disease.

15 ### They cleanse our atmosphere

Did you know that we also depend on trees to cleanse our atmosphere? They absorb the carbon dioxide that we breathe out, and provide the oxygen we need to breathe. In fact, around 10% of the world's oxygen is produced by the Amazon.

20 ### They help to prevent soil erosion

Tree roots hold the soil together, while the <u>canopy</u> protects the soil from heavy rains. If trees are removed from the forest, the unprotected soil is then simply washed away in heavy rains, causing blockages and floods in lowland rivers, while leaving
25 upland rivers dry.

They are the pharmacy of the world

It will astonish you to learn that more than 25% of our modern medicines <u>originate</u> from tropical forest plants. Even so, only an estimated 5–25% of all plant species have been discovered. 1,300 of
30 the known 2,000 cancer-fighting plants come from the rainforests.

So imagine the possibilities if we could experiment with the rest of the plants that are yet to be discovered. Rainforests could hold the cure to many diseases.

35 For all these reasons, large areas of healthy rainforest are essential to the life on our planet and it is vital that we protect them for future generations.

Source: www.rainforestconcern.org

Comprehension

A **Listen and respond**

1 What do the following figures relate to?

  a 30 million   **b** half   **c** two-thirds

2 List some of the things that might happen if we lose our rainforests.

B **Read and respond**

Answer the questions with your partner, giving evidence from the text to support your answers.

1 Match the underlined words in the text with the correct definitions below (a–g). Use the context to help you guess the meaning. When you have finished, use a dictionary to check your answers.

  a supplying crops with water

  b thick branches which make a sort of treetop ceiling

  c group of animals or plants that have the same features

  d plants and animals in a certain area

  e long periods of dry weather

  f originally come from

  g shortage of food

2 How does the rainforest affect the air we breathe?

3 Explain two ways that trees in the rainforest protect the soil beneath them.

4 What happens to the soil when large areas of trees are removed?

5 What estimated percentage of rainforest plants have been discovered?

● Compare fact and opinion

C **What do you think?**

1 What is the purpose of the following features?

   a the text as a whole

   b the first and last paragraphs

   c the subheadings

2 How would you describe the text?

   a mostly facts

   b mostly opinions

   c a mixture of facts and opinions

3 Find an example of:

   a one fact

   b one opinion

   c a question – why is it there?

   d a passive verb – why has it been used?

   e a conditional sentence – why has it been used?

   f a multi-clause sentence – find the subordinate clause and discuss the purpose of it

4 Summarise the second paragraph in less than 30 words.

5 Look up the meaning of the word 'transpiration'. Use the information in the text to help you explain this image to your partner.

?

Do you think we will manage to save the rainforests? Discuss what you could do to help protect the rainforests.

Stretch zone

Write a short text explaining the water cycle of a rainforest. Use the diagram to help you.

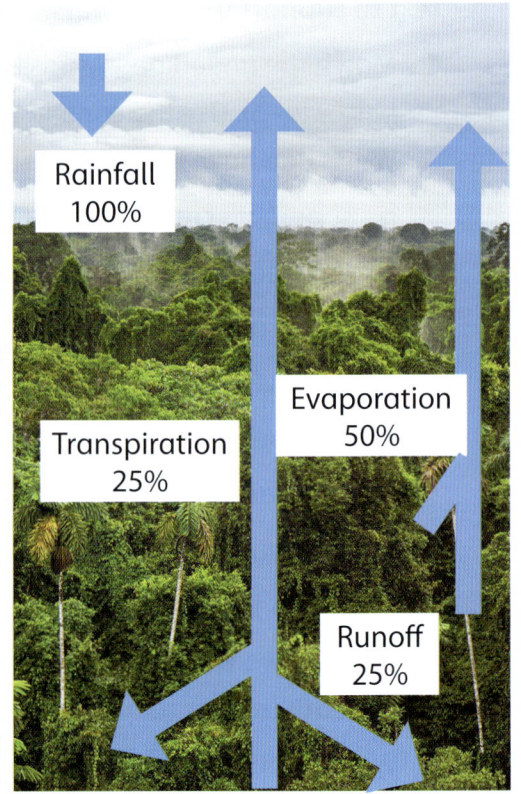

Rainfall 100%

Evaporation 50%

Transpiration 25%

Runoff 25%

Quantifiers

We use **quantifiers** when we want to give someone information about the number of something: how much or how many. There are three main types of quantifiers:

1 **Quantifiers for countable nouns.** *For example:* (not) many, each, either, (a) few, several, both, neither, fewer, a couple of.

   Examples: **Several** balls bounced over the fence.
   I gave **each** of my friends an invitation.

2 **Quantifiers for uncountable nouns.** *For example:* (not) much, a bit, a little, a great deal of (used with abstract nouns like time or money).

   Examples: We don't have **much** milk left.
   Nan gave her **a great deal of** money on her birthday.

3 **Quantifiers for both countable and uncountable nouns.** *For example:* all, some, more, a lot of, enough, any, most, lots of, less, plenty of.

   Examples: Laksari has **lots of** friends.
   Armeena has **plenty of** pencils. I can't go out – I've got **no** money.

A Complete these sentences with appropriate quantifiers.

1 You can choose that cake or that cake, but not _____ of them.

2 He likes _____ honey in his tea instead of sugar.

3 My granny has _____ pairs of glasses, but she still keeps losing them.

4 Add _____ drops of lemon juice to the cake mixture.

5 Lee was rushing. He didn't have _____ time because he needed to be back by 7pm.

B Complete these sentences with appropriate quantifiers.

1 Don't fight over the chocolates – there's _____ them in the box.

2 Have you got _____ money to pay for the bus fare?

3 Barney put _____ butter on his toast.

4 _____ the ice cream has been eaten – there's none left!

5 Make sure you pack _____ warm clothes – it's very cold.

We usually use the quantifier **some** in positive sentences and questions, and the quantifier **any** in negative sentences and questions.

Examples: We have **some** pets at home.

I saw **some** dolphins on holiday.

We don't have **any** pets.

I didn't see **any** dolphins on holiday.

We saw **some** iguanas at the zoo, but we didn't see **any** giant tortoises.

However, we can use **some** for offers and requests.

Examples: Would you like **some** squash?

I would like **some** water, please.

C Complete these sentences with **some** or **any**.

1 I don't have _____ felt tips to colour in the picture.

2 Do you want to borrow _____ of my felt tips?

3 I don't want _____ cake, thank you.

4 Please may I have _____ more cake?

 **Stretch zone**

Make a list of packages that we use as quantifiers when buying groceries.

For example: a bag of potatoes, a tin of chopped tomatoes.

Writing a non-chronological report

- Explore formal and informal language
- Understand the target audience

Read these three extracts about the effect of overfishing and the damage it has done to our oceans. The information in the extracts is similar but the style of writing is different.

1 We all know that, as well as being really tasty, fish is healthy. We also know that fish comes from the sea and there is plenty more where it came from, right? Sadly, this isn't the case. Until recently, our seas were brimming with fish, but they're disappearing. We don't see what happens in the ocean, so it's easy to forget or ignore the problem of overfishing – we just want to enjoy our fish! What's the problem then? Well, the bad news is that a recent study says that, unless we act quickly, there'll be no fish in the sea by 2048! That means that there may come a time in your lifetime when there'll be no fish for dinner! The good news is that we can do something about it: this can be stopped if we all play our part. One thing you can do is ask the adults in your house to buy fish from sustainable sources, which means that enough fish are left in the sea, and that the environment isn't damaged while fishing.

3 Overfishing is a relatively modern problem, and results from changes in the way we live. The first example of overfishing dates back to the 1800s, when whale blubber was used to power lamp oils, which had a significant impact on the number of whales in existence. In the 1900s, sardines, herring and Atlantic cod became popular to eat, and nearly became extinct as a result of overconsumption. Today, overfishing can be seen on a global scale, and this is having very serious repercussions on the food chain.

2 **Overfishing:** Overfishing happens when more of a fish species is caught and removed from the sea than can be replaced by the fish reproducing. The number of fish in the sea can also be affected by pollution, such as rubbish, oil and chemicals which end up in our waters.

A Look at each extract and answer the following questions.

1 Is the language formal or informal? How formal or informal is it?

2 Who is the target audience – adults? Teenagers? Young people your age?

3 Where might you read information like this? A newspaper? A magazine? A reference book? On the internet?

B **1** Use the information in the three extracts on page 141 to write a short summary about overfishing. What is it? Why it is happening? And what we can do about it? Write your summary in 60 words or less.

2 Compare your summary with your partner's. Can you reduce your summaries to 30 words or less and still answer the three questions above?

C **Before writing a report, you need to know who your target audience is. This will affect the formality of your writing.**

1 Look at the extracts about overfishing again. Make a list of the features of formal writing and the features of informal writing.

2 Look at the reports 'Last chance for Māui dolphins' on page 132 and 'Conserving rainforests' on page 136. Is the language formal or informal? Who do you think the target audiences are?

3 Both the reports on pages 132 and 136 are non-chronological reports. Using the reports to help you, make a list of the typical features of a non-chronological report.

Planning your report

You are going to write your own group report. Before you start, decide your roles in the group and who will be the group leader. You need to decide your topic – choose one that is connected to the environment and what you have been studying in other subjects at school.

Start by deciding which information each member of the group is researching. Remember you are summarising the information into note form.

Writing your report

1 Use the list of typical report features that you created earlier as success criteria to help you write your report from the notes. Make sure that you have a clear target audience in mind and that your language is appropriate. Organise your ideas into paragraphs with subheadings.

2 Once you have finished your report, check your work against your list of success criteria again to make sure you have used the key features of report writing. Does your text make sense and are your ideas presented in a logical order?

3 Check that the vocabulary, sentence structures and formality that you have used are appropriate for your target audience.

Making presentations in groups

4 Now present your report to the rest of the class. Make sure that each member of the group has a role in the presentation. When it is your turn to present, make sure that you speak confidently and vary your expression and tone to make your presentation more interesting.

A Smooth, scaly body **slithers** silently unseen through the tall grasses.

B

Isabel met an enormous bear,
Isabel, Isabel, didn't care;
The bear was hungry, the bear was ravenous,
The bear's big mouth was cruel and **cavernous**.
The bear said, Isabel, glad to meet you,
How do, Isabel, now I'll eat you!
Isabel, Isabel, didn't worry.
Isabel didn't scream or **scurry**.
She washed her hands and she straightened her hair up,
Then Isabel quietly ate the bear up.

From *Adventures of Isabel* by Ogden Nash

C

Wrinkly-stomper
Colossal-mover
Trunk-swinger
Trumpet-blower
Water-sprayer
Tusk-bearer
Ear-flapper

"Poetry is language at its most distilled and most powerful."
Rita Dove

Talk time

1 Is poetry an important or useful form of art?
2 Which is your favourite poem on these two pages?
3 What do you like about it?

Different forms of poetry

- Read a variety of poems
- Recognise different types of poems

Glossary

slithers slides across the ground

cavernous large, dark and empty, like a cave

scurry run quickly with short steps

colossal very big

incessantly continuing without stopping

anticipation feeling of expectation or hope

spatters splashes with small drops

D

There was an old man in a tree,
Whose whiskers were lovely to see;
But the birds of the air,
Pluck'd them perfectly bare,
To make themselves nests on that tree.

Edward Lear

E

"You are old, Father William," the young man said,
"And your hair has become very white;
And yet you **incessantly** stand on your head –
Do you think, at your age, it is right?"
"In my youth," Father William replied to his son,
"I feared it might injure the brain;
But, now that I'm perfectly sure I have none,
Why, I do it again and again."

From *Alice's Adventures in Wonderland* by Lewis Carroll

F

A
drop
of rain is
like a sudden
knock at the door.
Unexpected, yet often
welcomed with a smile. It
can brighten your day or ruin
your plans. It can make you laugh
or make you sad. Whether the raindrop
is moving fast or slow, or is big or small,
it always gets everyone's attention. A raindrop contains many secrets. It is a bubble of
anticipation and surprise. It cleanses the earth,
it feeds the flowers, and fills the holes. The
raindrop is never silent. It bangs on the
roof, **spatters** on the window, or
splashes into a puddle.
A raindrop.

Anonymous

- Recognise poetry features
- Practise reading poems aloud

A Match the poems (A–F) on pages 144 and 145 with the poem types (1–6) below.

1 A poem that is often silly or senseless, written in five lines with an AABBA rhyme scheme. It often tells a short, humorous story.

2 A poem which is composed of 3 lines, each a phrase. The first line typically has five syllables, the second line has seven and the last line has five.

3 A poem that describes an object and is shaped in the form of the object it is describing.

4 A poem made up of two-word phrases describing someone or something, using metaphorical language.

5 A poem that is specifically composed to be read out loud.

6 A poem that is a conversation between two characters, with each character expressing a different point of view.

B Read and respond

1 Poem A is describing an animal. Can you guess which animal? What literary technique is used in the poem? How does this imitate the animal it is describing?

2 Poem C is also describing an animal. Can you guess which one? Here are some more two-word phrases describing different animals. Can you guess which animal they are describing?

- Tummy-slider
- Head-twister
- Tree-swinger

3 Who are the two characters talking in the dialogue poem (E)? Why is one of them not worried about doing headstands?

4 Which word in poem B means 'very hungry'? Find all the end-of-line words and phrases which rhyme.

5 In poem F, explain why a raindrop is like a knock at the door. Find two examples of how a raindrop has a positive effect on the earth.

6 What was the old man's facial hair used for in poem D?

C In pairs, choose one of the poems to perform together. Decide how to make your performance interesting – by changing your expression and tone of voice and adding gestures.

• Understand compound words

Compound words

Raindrop is a **compound word**. A compound word is created when two or more words are combined to create a new word.

Examples: rain + drop = raindrop, foot + ball = football

Compound words can be written:

- as **one word**, such as newspaper, online, teapot
- as **hyphenated words**, such as one-third, eighty-six, daughter-in-law
- as **two words**, such as phone call, ice cream, post office.

A What one word can you add to all the words below to make new compound words?

brush   cut   spray   dresser   band   style

B Add one word from the list below to each of the words to make new compound words. The first one has been done for you.

fire   book   out   light   air   door   sand   sea   water

Example: __sand__ pit   __sand__ paper   __sand__ castle   __sand__ storm

1 _____plane	_____port	_____bag	_____line
2 _____shop	_____worm	_____shelf	_____mark
3 _____fighter	_____proof	_____place	_____fly
4 _____house	_____bulb	_____weight	_____headed
5 _____way	_____stop	_____mat	_____knob
6 _____food	_____horse	_____sick	_____shore
7 _____proof	_____colour	_____melon	_____fall
8 _____doors	_____let	_____number	_____law

C Write a list of all the different types of fly.

Example: firefly

- Understand rhyming patterns
- Write a shape poem

Shape poem

The Tornado

Swirling, twirling round and round,

sucking up the earth and ground.

Wind so strong and sky so black,

it will destroy all in its track.

Danger, danger, please beware,

because tornadoes

do not care.

Anonymous

Comprehension

A Read the poem. Then answer these questions, using words and phrases from the poem to support your answers.

1 Which words at the ends of lines rhyme?

2 Which words within the same line rhyme?

3 Which words are repeated in the same line and why?

B 1 List the four verbs that describe what a tornado does.

2 How does the shape of the poem help you understand it and experience the language?

C Write a shape poem of your own. Choose one of these topics.

| flood | wave | volcano | tornado |

1 First, draw the outline of your shape poem.

2 Find some ideas below to help you.

a hurling hot rocks at the sky in noisy anger / dirtying the land, covering fields with dust / pouring hot lava from the corners of its mouth ...

b racing silently across the ocean / feeling the seabed scraping along its belly / rising to greet the tree-lined shore ...

c circling the centre of the city / bending trees ...

Stretch zone

Write a limerick (poem D, page 145) starting with the first line 'There was a young boy/girl from _____ (the name of your country)'.

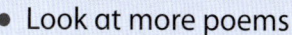

- Look at more poems
- Understand meaning in poems

It's only the storm

'What's that creature that rattles the roof?'
2 'Hush, it's only the storm.'
'What's blowing the tiles and the branches off?'
4 'Hush, it's only the storm.'
'What's riding the sky like a wild white horse,
6 Flashing its teeth and stamping its hooves?'
'Hush, my dear, it's only the storm,
8 Racing the darkness till it catches the dawn.
Hush, my dear, it's only the storm,
10 When you wake in the morning, it will be gone.'

David Greygoose

Comprehension

A Read the poem. Then answer these questions, using words and phrases from the poem to support your answers.

1 What is happening in the poem?

2 Is it night time or day time?

3 Who do you think are the two people talking in the poem?

B Answer these questions, using the poem to help you.

1 Why is the line 'Hush, it's only the storm' repeated? Why does that line then change to 'Hush, **my dear**, it's only the storm'?

2 How does the poet build up the feeling of the child's fear in the poem?

3 Find examples of: alliteration, a metaphor, a simile and a rhyme.

C 1 Write some more verses to the poem by asking questions about the storm using figurative language.

Example: What's pummelling the windows and slamming the doors?

Hush, it's only the storm.

What's raging through the sky like a stampeding bull?

Hush, it's only the storm.

2 Write another poem titled *It's only the rain*. Use figurative language to describe the noise of heavy rain.

149

- Revise speech marks in dialogue
- Use dialogue punctuation correctly

Revising speech marks

"You are old, Father William," the young man said,
"And your hair has become very white;
And yet you incessantly stand on your head –
Do you think, at your age, it is right?"

"In my youth," Father William replied to his son,
"I feared it might injure the brain;
But, now that I'm perfectly sure I have none,
Why, I do it again and again."

From *Alice's Adventures in Wonderland* by Lewis Carroll

A Using the dialogue from the poem, write out the rules for:
- using speech marks when someone is speaking
- where commas should be placed when speech marks are used
- when someone speaking asks a question
- what to do when someone new speaks
- what to do when the speech is 'interrupted' by a reporting clause.

B Write out the following passage, correcting the errors and setting out the dialogue properly.

Are you coming out tonight? Alexa asked. No, I can't replied Sabrina. I have football training. Do you want to come and watch the training session? No thanks, Alexa replied, feeling really disappointed. She had wanted Sabrina to come out with her tonight. It was her birthday after all. Alexa folded her arms and looked at her friend sadly. Oh, come on Alexa, don't be cross replied Sabrina. Let's go out afterwards. How about it?

- Learn different ways of spelling the same sound

Same sounds, different spellings

Spelling the /k/ sound

A Can you remember the different ways of spelling the /k/ sound? Use the following words to help you:

cat   unique   make   hook   sack

Spelling the /ch/ sound

The /ch/ sound can be written **-ch** or **-tch**.

- If the final /ch/ sound comes after a consonant, the ending is **-ch**, such as lun**ch**, ben**ch** and per**ch**.
- If the final /ch/ sound follows a one-letter vowel, it is usually written **-tch**, for example: ca**tch**, clu**tch**, i**tch** and stre**tch**.
- There are exceptions to this rule, for example: attach, much, which, rich and such.
- If the final /ch/ sound comes after a two-letter vowel, the ending should be spelt **-ch**, such as bea**ch**, spee**ch**, poa**ch** and ou**ch**.

B Write the correct ending (**-ch** or **-tch**) to the following words.

scra_____   tea_____   swi_____   pea_____   ma_____
pou_____   brun_____   pa_____   sti_____   bun_____

Spelling the /j/ sound

If the /j/ sound is followed by a vowel (**a, e, i, o** or **u**), we usually use the letter **j**. For example, **j**am, **j**elly or **j**ockey.

The letter **g** can make the /j/ sound when it is followed by an **e, i**, or **y** as in **ge**sture, **gi**nger or **gy**m.

If /j/ follows a short vowel sound, we usually use **dge** as in dodge or wedge.

C 1 Write three more words that use **j** to make the /j/ sound.

2 Write three more words that use **g** to make the /j/ sound.

3 Write one more word that uses **dge** to make the /j/ sound.

 **Stretch zone**

Keep a list of words that end in a /k/ sound. Sort them into different spelling columns to help you remember them.

Kennings

- Discuss writer's choice of vocabulary
- Explore kennings

In these poems, the lines are made up of two words joined together with a hyphen, making a new word. These are kennings. The 'Historian' poem uses kennings to describe the different ways of being a historian (someone who studies the past). Use a dictionary to look up any unfamiliar words.

Glossary

rune letter of the alphabet used in the past
parchment old-fashioned writing paper
hounder hunter
bearer holder

Historian

Time-detective
Bone-collector
Stone-saver
Rune-reader
5 **Parchment**-keeper
Villain-**hounder**
Hero-maker
Grave-digger
Fact-hunter
10 Story-searcher
Truth-seeker
Year-counter
Age-teller
Past-banker

John Kitching

An archaeologist at a dig

Who is this?

Stripey-starer
Eyeline-wearer
Hook-holder
Snake-**bearer**
5 Beard-plaiter
Necklace-prisoner
Gold-giver
Gold-taker

Eleanor Watts

Comprehension

A Answer these questions, using the poem to help you.

1 In the poem 'Historian', find joined-up words that could mean:

   a a historian who likes a person from history

   b a historian who dislikes a person from history

2 Explain why the poet calls a historian:

   a time-detective   b rune-reader

3 Kennings often use alliteration, as in **s**tone-**s**aver.
   Find one more example of alliteration in 'Historian'.

B Answer these questions, using the poem to help you.

1 The poem 'Who is this?' on page 152 is about a pharaoh.
   Use your dictionary to look up this word.

2 Why do you think the pharaoh is called a 'necklace-prisoner'?

3 Who do you think the pharaoh gives gold to and takes gold from?

4 Read the poem below. Describe to your partner some of the things
   this person does. Do you know somebody who does these things
   for you? Who do you think is being described?

Who is this?

Nightmare-wiper	Story-teller
Morning-waker	10 Problem-solver
Sock-finder	Love-giver
5 Lunchbox-maker	Wise-worrier
Hair-comber	Life-giver
Quarrel-queller	Eleanor Watts
School-runner	

C 1 Write your own short kenning poem of 4 or 5 lines about a job,
   such as a teacher, doctor or nurse. Use pairs of joined-up words
   and try to use alliteration.

2 Read your kenning poem aloud. Ask your class to guess who
   your poem describes.

● Look at different poetic techniques

My Dad's a Secret Agent

My dad's a secret agent.
He's an undercover spy.
He's the world's best detective.
4 He's the perfect private eye.

He's a **Pinkerton**, a **gumshoe**,
He's a snoop and he's a sleuth.
He's **unrivalled** at detecting
8 and uncovering the truth.

He's got eyesight like an eagle.
He's got hearing like a bat.
He can out-smell any **bloodhound**.
12 He's as stealthy as a cat.

He can locate nearly anything
with **elementary** ease.
But no matter how he looks and looks
16 my dad can't find his keys!

Kenn Nesbitt

Glossary

Pinkerton, gumshoe slang words for investigator or detective
unrivalled the best at something
bloodhound dog who uses its nose to follow a scent
elementary simple

The Pinkerton National Detective Agency was founded in the USA in 1850. This is the original logo.

Comprehension

A **Answer these questions, giving evidence from the poem to support your answers.**

1 Find three other words in the poem that mean 'spy'.

2 Find three examples where you think the poet is exaggerating the abilities of his dad.

3 Why has the poet decided to leave the fact that his dad cannot find his keys until the last line?

B **1** Which two of the techniques below has the poet *not* used?

   a alliteration   **d** every line rhymes

   b simile   **e** repeated words

   c kennings

2 Find examples in the poem to illustrate two of the techniques the poet did use.

3 Why has the poet used an exclamation mark at the end?

Poetry performance and writing workshop

1   In groups, read the poem on page 154 together.

- Practise reading it aloud together, using rhythm for emphasis.

- Now, each person read a line aloud in turn.

- All together, read the first verse aloud quietly, then get louder towards the end of the poem.

2   Remain working in your group. Using the vocabulary from 'My Dad's a Secret Agent' to help you, and your own ideas, write a kenning poem about what it is like being a spy. Make your poem between 10 and 15 lines long.

3   Once you are all satisfied with your final version, practise reading your poem in your group. Decide how you are going to present your poem to the class. Are you going to say separate lines or recite the poem together as a group? Are you going to use movement or gestures as you recite the lines? Are you going to alternate the tone and the volume of your voices?

4   As a class, listen to all the groups present their reading of their poem. Give feedback about the choice of language and the presentation of the new poems.

Revise and check (3)

Vocabulary

1 **Complete the shopping list by adding a suitable quantifier.**

a <u>bag</u> of apples

a _____ of sugar   a _____ of orange juice

a _____ of milk   a _____ of bread

a _____ of dog food   a _____ of eggs

a _____ of oil   a _____ of butter

2 **Write compound words beginning with the following parts of the body.**

hand_____   hand_____   hand_____

arm_____   arm_____   arm_____

ear_____   ear_____   ear_____

eye_____   eye_____   eye_____

head_____   head_____   head_____

Poems and figurative language

1 **Write down the names of four different kinds of poem.**

2 **Write out the sentences below, adding the correct idiom from the list.**

> to cut a long story short   from scratch   speaking my mind
> tip of my tongue   rings a bell   no-brainer

a I made the cake _____.

b Football or homework? It's a _____! I'm playing football.

c _____, I broke my leg when I was ice-skating.

d Sometimes I get into trouble for _____ without thinking.

e I can't remember her name but it's on the _____.

f Was it Lee Chong Wei? I'm not certain but the name _____.

Punctuation

1 **Punctuate the dialogue below. Start a new line every time the speaker changes.**

Hello Achieng. Hello Jacob. Did you have a good holiday? Great, thanks. We went to Mombasa to see my auntie. Did you stay there for the whole holiday? No, I had to help my mother in our shop in Nairobi for four weeks.

Grammar

1 **Change these sentences from passive to active.**

   a Dinner is usually prepared by her father.

   b The visitors were frightened by the howling wolves.

   c The package has been delivered by the delivery driver.

2 **Write out the passive form of these sentences.**

   a The children (take) to the party by their parents.

   b The new gym (opened) by a famous footballer.

3 **Complete the instructions by using a suitable imperative verb.**

_____ the sugar and _____ together with a wooden spoon. After a few minutes, the mixture should be creamy. _____ the eggs, one by one, and continue mixing. _____ in the flour carefully. _____ the mixture into a tin and _____ in the oven for 35 minutes.

4 **Write an example of a single-clause sentence and a multi-clause sentence.**

Spelling

1 **Write a sentence which includes each pair of homophones.**

   a their there

   b meat meet

   c knows nose

   d flower flour

2 **Write two words with two different /ch/ sound endings.**

3 **Write two words with two different /j/ sound endings.**

Adventures of Isabel

Isabel met an enormous bear,
Isabel, Isabel, didn't care;
The bear was hungry, the bear was ravenous,
The bear's big mouth was cruel and cavernous.
5 The bear said, Isabel, glad to meet you,
How do, Isabel, now I'll eat you!
Isabel, Isabel, didn't worry.
Isabel didn't scream or scurry.
She washed her hands and she straightened her hair up,
10 Then Isabel quietly ate the bear up.

Once in a night as black as **pitch**
Isabel met a wicked old witch.
The witch's face was cross and wrinkled,
The witch's gums with teeth were sprinkled.
15 Ho, ho, Isabel! The old witch **crowed**,
I'll turn you into an ugly toad!
Isabel, Isabel, didn't worry,
Isabel didn't scream or scurry,
She showed no rage and she showed no **rancour**,
20 But she turned the witch into milk and drank her.

Isabel met a hideous giant,
Isabel continued **self reliant**.
The giant was hairy, the giant was horrid,
He had one eye in the middle of his forehead.
25 Good morning, Isabel, the giant said,
I'll grind your bones to make my bread.
Isabel, Isabel, didn't worry,
Isabel didn't scream or scurry.
She nibbled the **zwieback** that she always fed off,
30 And when it was gone, she cut the giant's head off.

Isabel met a troublesome doctor,
He punched and he poked till he really shocked her.
The doctor's talk was of coughs and chills
And the doctor's **satchel** bulged with pills.
35 The doctor said unto Isabel,
Swallow this, it will make you well.
Isabel, Isabel, didn't worry,
Isabel didn't scream or scurry.
She took those pills from the pill **concocter**,
40 And Isabel calmly cured the doctor.

Ogden Nash

The 'Veggy' Lion

I'm a vegetarian lion,
I've given up all meat,
I've given up roaring
4 All I do is go tweet-tweet.

I never ever sink my claws
Into some animal's skin,
It only lets the blood run out
8 And lets the germs rush in.

I used to be ferocious,
I even tried to kill!
But the sight of all that blood
12 Made me feel quite ill.

I once attacked an elephant
I sprang straight at his head.
I woke up three days later
16 In a jungle hospital bed.

Now I just eat carrots,
They're easier to kill,
'Cos when I pounce upon them,
20 They all remain quite still!

Spike Milligan